OECD INSIGHTS

Economic Globalisation

Origins and Consequences

Jean-Yves Huwart and Loïc Verdier

BETTER POLICIES FOR BETTER LIVES

This work is published on the responsibility of the Secretary-General of the OECD. The opinions expressed and arguments employed herein do not necessarily reflect the official views of the Organisation or of the governments of its member countries.

This document and any map included herein are without prejudice to the status of or sovereignty over any territory, to the delimitation of international frontiers and boundaries and to the name of any territory, city or area.

Please cite this publication as:
Huwart, J.Y. and L. Verdier (2013), *Economic Globalisation: Origins and Consequences*, OECD Insights, OECD Publishing.
http://dx.doi.org/10.1787/9789264111899-en

ISBN 978-92-64-11189-9 (print)
ISBN 978-92-64-11190-5 (PDF)

Series: OECD Insights
ISSN 1993-6745 (print)
ISSN 1993-6753 (online)

The statistical data for Israel are supplied by and under the responsibility of the relevant Israeli authorities. The use of such data by the OECD is without prejudice to the status of the Golan Heights, East Jerusalem and Israeli settlements in the West Bank under the terms of international law.

Photo credits: Cover © Photoredaktor/Dreamstime.com
pp. 10-11 © adisa/Fotolia
pp. 18-19: © Slava Gerjv/Shutterstock.com.
pp. 32-33: © Sergej Seemann/Fotolia
pp. 48-49: © Engine Images/Fotolia
pp. 68-69: © africa924/Shutterstock.com.
pp. 88-89: © BartlomiejMagierowski/Shutterstock.com.
pp. 108-109: © catscandotcom /iStockphoto
pp. 126-127: © Ryan McVay/Getty

Corrigenda to OECD publications may be found on line at: *www.oecd.org/publishing/corrigenda*.

Foreword

International trade, migration and globalised finance are the ingredients of a cocktail named globalisation, the recipe of which we haven't yet mastered and the taste of which we may, if we're not careful, find bitter.

Furthermore, these three ingredients are very unevenly dosed. Most countries want to strictly control international migration. They're making timid efforts to organise international trade (booming since containerisation) in major negotiations, while finance – globalisation's most successful component – is still regulated very weakly.

It's an explosive mixture. Governments face widely-varying obstacles depending on migrants' qualifications and country of origin, against the backdrop of a social question that's becoming global. Trade growth creating both winners and, lest it be forgotten, losers is a source of tension. The economy's excessive "financialisation" has emerged as the ideal culprit for a crisis whose extent we're only now starting to measure, and runs the risk of distracting attention from a whole set of imbalances that have been growing over the past 20 years.

The danger lies in making globalisation responsible for most rich countries' economic ills – offshoring, de-industrialisation, unemployment, rising income inequality, impoverished remote regions, and standardised lifestyles – and deluding us into believing that if we can reverse the phenomenon, we will solve all these problems.

The truth is that no simple solution such as "deglobalisation" can respond to such complex phenomena. This book's great merit is that it summarises currently available analyses and provides benchmarks against which we can evaluate the effectiveness of our judgments and policies in overcoming the growing fragility of individuals, companies, sectors, countries, and sometimes even entire regions.

To support these benchmarks, the book provides an extensive historical overview that shows how empires and trade grew side by side. Where previously we had a centre and a periphery, today we are witnessing the emergence of a multi-centric world economy and the increasingly pronounced convergence of emerging countries, led by China, India and Brazil.

While this convergence is specific to globalisation (on the upswing in the past 30 years), it also applies to life expectancy, fertility and – quite spectacularly – education. Between the early 1960s and 2010, the literacy rate of the world population increased from under 60% to 82%. This crucial aspect of "immaterial" globalisation is the combined result of generalised schooling, widespread communication networks and the proliferation of media for exchanging information.

Our view of globalisation is very much influenced by the angle from which we approach it. I would like to emphasise three of the issues covered in this book. First, we must be very careful with the numbers we use to measure globalisation. Statistics are misleading. Trade is conducted by companies, not countries. Some of what features in international flows is only intra-firm trade stemming from a globally dispersed value chain, and some of what features in domestic flows stems from the activities of subsidiaries belonging to foreign groups that have decided to shift from exporting to producing in the local market. Yet while this features in companies' international activities, it mostly does not appear in international flows.

Further, in the interests of objectivity, we need to retain a certain perspective on the extent of global economic integration. As Matthieu Crozet and Lionel Fontagné reminded us in Économie et statistiques (Economy and Statistics), published by the National Institute of Statistics and Economic Studies (INSEE) in 2010: "In developed and emerging countries alike, the share of companies directly engaged in an international relationship is very much the minority, and rarely exceeds 20%. Moreover, most exporters have an extremely limited presence in global markets and are active only in a small number of neighbouring markets."

Finally, while most globalisation studies cover the legal economy, what do we know of the extent of the "dark side" of globalisation – the black market economy, offshore centres, etc.? As Alain Bauer and Xavier Raufer wrote in La face noire de la mondialisation (The Dark Side of Globalisation), published by the Centre national de la recherche scientifique (CNRS) in 2009, we must examine "how this criminal globalisation undermines economies, finances, and countries" if we are to implement effective policies to combat practices and organisations that undermine democracies and equitable economies.

It is up to each of us to observe and gauge, curiously and cautiously, the magnitude of the complex phenomenon of globalisation.

Pascal Le Merrer

Economist, professor at the École normale supérieure de Lyon, author of *Économie de la mondialisation: opportunités et fractures* (The Economics of Globalisation: Opportunities and Fractures) (de Boeck, Brussels, 2007)

Acknowledgments

The authors wish to thank Brian Keeley and Patrick Love for their editorial contribution and the following for their valuable advice and participation: Adrian Blundell-Wignall, Brendan Gillespie, Przemyslaw Kowalski, Andrew Mold, Raed Safadi and Paul Swaim.

We particularly wish to thank Katherine Kraig-Ernandes, Clare O'Hare-d'Armagnac, Jean Mispelblom Beijer and Janine Treves.

The book was translated from French by Romy de Courtay and copyedited by Peter Coles.

OECD Insights Blog : *http://oecdinsights.org.*

OECD Insights is a series of primers commissioned by the OECD Public Affairs and Communications Directorate. They draw on the Organisation's research and expertise to introduce and explain some of today's most pressing social and economic issues to non-specialist readers.

TABLE OF CONTENTS

Currency note

Currency references are in US dollars unless otherwise indicated.

This book has...

StatLinks

A service that delivers Excel® files from the printed page!

Look for the *StatLinks* at the bottom right-hand corner of the tables or graphs in this book.
To download the matching Excel® spreadsheet, just type the link into your Internet browser,
starting with the *http://dx.doi.org* prefix.
If you're reading the PDF e-book edition, and your PC is connected to the Internet, simply
click on the link. You'll find *StatLinks* appearing in more OECD books.

1

Economic globalisation is highly controversial – even more so since the recent global economic crisis. "Pro-globalists" and "anti-globalists" (also known as "alter-globalists") have hotly debated the issue for a good twenty years. Most of this planet's inhabitants experience some of the considerable benefits and also the tragic downside of globalisation in their daily lives. It is essential to trace the history of this complex phenomenon and the various forms it takes if we want to tackle the challenges it brings in its wake.

Introduction

By way of introduction...

Madrid, May 2011. Summer hasn't begun, but looks set to be a scorcher. In a tapas bar on a shady street somewhere between the Plaza del Sol and the Avenida de Mostoles, Rodrigo, the owner, tidies up. A couple sits next to the window, chatting in a Slavic tongue.

At the back, between the wooden chairs and an oversized black-and-white photograph of a bullfight, a refrigerated wine cellar hums softly, a Haier label proudly displayed on its stainless steel door. Rodrigo slides in a dozen bottles of red wine, some of which come from Chile's Maipo Valley. He serves the seated customers a pot of Tetley tea with the label hanging down the side. He clears another table, then heads into the kitchen and aligns three dirty glasses in the Beko dishwasher. Several cards stick out of his wallet under the counter, including one bearing the red-and-white logo of the Lukoil petrol chain.

Today, the Spanish capital seems busier than usual. Several hundred people dressed in yellow blow foghorns and whistles on the street. They brandish banners calling for the re-opening of the electrical appliances factory where they used to work. Caught up by the crisis, the Swedish parent company has given up on its plan to invest in its La Mancha facility. Instead, it intends to move production to its existing plants in Romania and Morocco. The workers are demanding that management reconsider.

On the pavement next to the march, several hundred young members of the *"Indignados"* ("Outraged") movement hand out flyers demanding a tax on the profits of the world's largest multinational enterprises (MNEs), an end to financial speculation, draconian limits on traders' bonuses, and a levy on international transactions. The September 2008 financial crisis brought the global economic machine to an abrupt halt and affected all of the world economies more or less deeply. News programmes are filled with personal tragedies.

Rodrigo is also feeling the effects of the crisis. Until recently, his tapas bar was chugging along nicely, thanks to an influx of tourists from Russia, Brazil and Chile, and even from as far off as China and India. Only a year ago, Rodrigo hung a "Welcome" sign on his door in Cyrillic and Chinese. But business ground to a halt as the ensuing economic crisis triggered a drastic drop in tourism.

That's not all. At the time, Rodrigo had decided to expand his business by purchasing the premises next door. At first, the bank looked favourably on his project. But the subprime bubble burst (subprimes are loans secured by very fragile mortgages in the United States), hitting all of the world's major banks. Eight thousand kilometres away from the poor US households whose homes were being seized by the banks, Rodrigo's credit manager greeted him in his central Madrid office with a grimace: "Sorry, but we need more guarantees. We've tightened our lending criteria."

"What a shame! I'll do the extension some other time", says Rodrigo to himself later, as he gazes through the window at the cluster of young protesters locked in a heated argument outside. One of them takes a snapshot of the protest with his Samsung mobile phone.

What kind of globalisation?

This scene could have taken place in almost any OECD country. It illustrates the many dimensions of economic globalisation: the increased movement of people across borders, in this particular case through tourism; the growing everyday use of products sourced around the world, particularly in emerging countries (see box below); the changes in corporate strategies based on the international presence of firms, and their potential impact on employment; and finally, the rapid global spread of an initially localised crisis. In other words, the deployment of people, goods, economic activity and money across national borders.

In his book *Globalization and its Discontents,* economist Joseph Stiglitz defines economic globalisation as "... the closer integration of the countries and peoples of the world which has been brought about by the enormous reduction of costs of transportation and communication, and the breaking down of artificial barriers to the flows of goods, services, capital, knowledge, and (to a lesser extent) people across borders".

This definition helps clarify what has become a "catch-all" term. For most people, "globalisation" refers to very diverse phenomena, such as informational, cultural, or political globalisation. This book mainly covers the *economic* consequences of globalisation: the increased international trade in goods and services, of course, but also the evolution of MNEs, the organisation of industrial production across borders, and the global crisscrossing of workers and students spurred by economic need. The financial and economic crisis that erupted in 2008 also makes it particularly important to analyse financial globalisation – an increasingly significant aspect of economic globalisation.

Addressing these issues also means discussing certain features of political globalisation. For the past decades, economic globalisation has been shaped in part by the collective decisions of world governments, often taken within the context of international organisations – the International Monetary Fund (IMF), World Bank, World Trade Organization (WTO), OECD, and so on – which monitor and evaluate its evolutions.

Economic globalisation has a growing influence on our lifestyles, our ways of working and our aspirations. For a few months, the economic crisis seemed to have stopped it dead. But since late 2009 or so, global trade and investment have recovered the momentum of the early 1990s, when the formerly communist countries opened up to international trade and the market economy. For better and (sometimes) for worse, globalisation is having a profound and lasting influence on the fate of modern societies.

A highly controversial phenomenon

Few subjects are as controversial as globalisation, particularly when it comes to its economic – and now financial – impact. Those who support it point to the vast array of new products, greater choices and cheaper goods for consumers, owing to intense international competition – not to mention technological advances, greater comfort and ease of everyday life, expanded leisure time, etc. Its opponents see globalisation as an unequal and biased process that destroys jobs and promotes economic imbalances, as well as excessive consumerism and major environmental damage from unbridled trade.

Even before the economic crisis (more precisely, between 31 October 2007 and 25 January 2008) London's BBC World Service conducted a poll of 34 000 individuals in 34 countries on what globalisation meant to them. The results reflected a generalised malaise. In 22 countries, the majority of respondents felt that the globalisation process was happening too quickly. "Many want to slow down – as opposed to stop – the movement", the BBC reported. In one-third of the countries (particularly China, India, Canada, Australia, United Arab Emirates, and Russia), they felt that globalisation brought improvements over previous economic situations. In two-thirds of the remaining countries (including Italy, the Philippines, Indonesia, the United States and Portugal), on the contrary, they believed their situation was worsening. Also, in only seven countries (United Arab Emirates, Australia, United States, China, Ghana, Nigeria, and Canada) did they consider the ongoing process of globalisation as balanced and transparent.

People worry about many things: the transfer of production to low-cost countries, the lack of job security, the volatility of raw materials prices, the loss of control over a series of economic levers, etc. Yet their perceptions of the impact of globalisation are sometimes far removed from its actual effects. Globalisation harbours a number of preconceptions, which foster a feeling of anxiety – particularly in industrialised countries.

What this book is about

The goal of this book is to assess globalisation as objectively as possible, drawing on OECD data and analyses and other reliable sources.

We begin with an **explanation of global economic integration,** tracing its history and briefly describing its extent today:

▶ Chapter 2 examines the historical milestones that both facilitated and exacerbated economic interactions among countries and peoples until they were interrupted by the Second World War. The idea of economic globalisation is rooted in rich and ancient history. The great discoveries of the 15th century and the Industrial Revolution of the 19th century accelerated global economic integration, while the protectionism of the Great Depression in the 1930s slowed it down and even reversed it.

▶ Chapter 3 shows how Western economic integration grew stronger after the Second World War, thanks both to the dynamism of business following the reconstruction and the institutional process of liberalising international trade. Yet the world remained economically fragmented until the early 1990s, due to very limited trade between Western and communist bloc countries.

▶ Chapter 4 describes the globalisation process since the 1990s, in the sense most commonly understood, stemming from two major phenomena: the opening of the large, formerly communist countries to international markets and the new information and communication technologies (ICT) revolution. It examines the way globalisation has gained pace over the past 20 years, studying in turn the (particularly developed) globalisation of goods and capital and the globalisation of services and people (in many respects, still in its infancy). It will also attempt to assess how globalised the world economy is today.

The second part of this book evaluates the current effects of global-isation and analyses its impact on four crucial sectors: employment, development, environment and financial stability.

▶ Chapter 5 studies the impact of globalisation on development. Some countries (particularly emerging economies) have clearly benefited from globalisation. But for others, its impact on their overall development, as well as on their poverty and inequality levels – in other words, on their people – isn't so clear-cut.

▶ Chapter 6 mainly considers to what extent globalisation destroys or creates jobs in Western countries, as well as its impact on job quality.

▶ Chapter 7 examines the impact of globalisation on the environment. The upsurge in cross-border trade and economic activities, combined with increasingly internationalised modes of production and consumption, can cause extensive environmental damage. But globalisation itself can offer some solutions.

▶ Chapter 8 deals with financial stability, examining the shock wave triggered by the 2007-08 financial crisis, considered the first great financial crisis of the global economy. At the time of writing, the bumpy road to recovery casts some doubt on the future of globalisation.

Some new faces
of the globalised economy

Ten years ago, none of the brands mentioned at the beginning of this chapter were found outside of their country of origin. They have in common the fact that they originated in an "emerging" country. In the 1980s, only Harrods department store in London – famous for being able to get hold of any article, anywhere – could bring together products from countries as varied as Chile, India, Turkey, the former Soviet Union, South Africa and Korea. In 2009, a simple Spanish tavern could bring them all together in one place, something that's common today, demonstrating the economic surge of emerging countries.

Haier

Created in 1984, the Chinese group Haier is the fourth-largest global producer of household appliances and the leader in a few product categories, including refrigerated wine cellars, freezers, air conditioners, washing machines and vacuum cleaners. It has more recently diversified into making audiovisual, computing and telecommunications equipment, not to mention a pharmaceuticals branch and has entered the services sector. With a cutting-edge innovation policy worthy of major European or Japanese manufacturers, the group posted a turnover of USD 23 billion in 2011, exports to 165 countries and operates 30 manufacturing plants around the world.

Arçelik

Turkey's Beko has a similar background to Haier's. In 2009, the company sold 8 million units (refrigerators, dishwashers, etc.). Its parent company, Arçelik, is now the third-largest manufacturer of household appliances in Europe.

Tata

Since 2000, Tetley Tea has been owned by the Indian conglomerate Tata, an old family-run industrial group created in the 19th century. Carried on the winds of globalisation, the South-Asian giant has regularly been in the news, whether purchasing the Anglo-Dutch steelworks company Corus in 2007, or the car manufacturer Jaguar in 2008, or launching the very low-cost (USD 2 000) Nano car.

Samsung

In 1960, the gross domestic product (GDP) per capita in South Korea was lower than in sub-Saharan Africa. Less than half a century later, one of its jewels, Samsung, is among the most dynamic companies in the world and the second-largest producer of mobile phones, ahead of US manufacturer Motorola.

Lukoil

Just over 10 years after the fall of the USSR, the Russian Federation's top oil company has developed its activities on all five continents. Soon, its international distribution network will be on a par with other renowned oil companies, Shell, Total or Exxon. American, Belgian or Romanian drivers can now fill up at a Lukoil petrol station.

Chilean wines

The global adventure for Chilean wines began many years ago and today they are on tables all around the world. In 10 years, sales have practically doubled and Santiago now ranks fifth among top wine exporters, ahead of countries with a strong winemaking tradition, such as Germany or Portugal. Thanks to an international communication campaign, Chilean producers have improved the image of their wines around the world, to the delight of Spanish, European and American aficionados.

2

AMERICA SEPTENTRIONALIS

MARE CARIBIVM

OCEA

COLVMBVS PRIMVS INVENTOR

COL

Economic globalisation in the broadest sense is as ancient as commercial trade. It resulted from a combination of dynamic merchants seeking new markets outside their own borders, improved transportation and communication techniques, and political desire to foster foreign trade – all of which occurred to different degrees at different points in time over the centuries.

The merchant, the inventor and the sovereign

PRIMA COLVMBI
IN INDIAM
NAVIGATIO

AFRICA

VS ATLANTICVS

ABVS

By way of introduction...

> **"Before, the events that took place in the world were not linked. Now, they are all dependent on each other."**
>
> Polybius, 2nd century BC

In light of this surprising statement by Greek historian Polybius, economic globalisation is clearly not something new. Long before Greek civilisation, there was already some economic interdependence between peoples. During the Neolithic (the dawn of agriculture), communities living hundreds of miles apart traded among themselves. As early as 7000 BC, one of the first known cities, Çatal Hüyük (now located in current-day Turkey), traded vast amounts of the volcanic stone obsidian, used in tool-making, against pottery and cereals from various peoples of the coastal Mediterranean.

Merchants from far and wide crossed paths during the time of the "Fertile Crescent". During the 3rd and 4th millennia BC, the Mesopotamian civilisation engaged in major trade (in metals, wood, building stone, etc.) with its neighbours Syria and Anatolia, then India and the Persian Gulf. Similarly, Egyptian pharaohs sent their caravans, vessels and scribes deep into their territories, from Phoenicia and Nubia to the Country of Pount (now in Eritrea).

So is economic globalisation as ancient as economic activity itself? Yes, if globalisation is taken to mean the economic interdependence of geographically distinct peoples. Only after the "Age of Discovery" of the 15th and 16th centuries did it come to mean the economic integration of the five continents. As for "globalisation" in the sense of participation by a majority of world states in the market economy and free trade, this only began in the early 1990s.

Even in the larger sense, economic globalisation has not been a linear historical process. It has sped up, slowed down, and sometimes screeched to a halt. As we will see in the first three chapters, its phases of acceleration have followed each other at an increasingly rapid pace, fuelled mostly by three factors: commercial dynamism, technological advances in transportation and communication, and political desire to foster foreign trade.

The origins of economic globalisation (from Antiquity to the 14th century)

The dynamism of international trade in Antiquity and the Middle Ages was helped by well-known transportation and communication techniques that are easily underestimated. The two essential inventions that spurred trade were shipping and writing. Certainly, animals that could carry goods over long hauls, such as horses and camels, had been domesticated well before then. The invention of the wheel during the 4th century BC in Mesopotamia also marked a turning point, by increasing the volume of goods that could be carried over long distances. But shipping gave the greatest boost to international trade, and still carries the largest quantities of freight around the world today.

Writing is intimately linked to economics and trade, too. Its oldest form – also invented in Mesopotamia in the 4th century BC – was initially used to record livestock and harvests, then written legal contracts, which were particularly important to make sure transactions were carried through over long distances. While this legal safety net fostered trade between geographically distant areas, the merchants' physical safety was even more essential. This is where politics comes in.

Empires and "world economies"

The first forms of globalisation are linked in part to the great empires that, by politically unifying very vast and disparate territories, enhanced the movement of goods and people across continents. From the 6th to the 4th century BC, merchants crisscrossed the vast Persian Empire, which spread from the Mediterranean to the River Ganges and covered a mosaic of peoples and civilisations. Its successor, Alexander the Great's Macedonian Empire, also linked the East and the West, pushing the borders even farther apart. This period of cultural integration of disparate peoples (demonstrated by the Great Library of Alexandria) also spread trading techniques, like the use of currency. The city-states of the post-Macedonian Hellenistic civilisation took advantage of the expanded borders and continued to engage heavily in (essentially maritime) trade.

Heir to the Greeks, the Roman Empire (5th century BC-5th century AD) also covered an immense geographic area, from

Scotland to Egypt and Spain to Asia Minor, which some historians consider the first "globalised" area. Thriving trade among extremely disparate regions benefited both from a very effective administration and major technological innovations. The network of roads and bridges, the expanded use of currency and the first sophisticated postal services increased trade and population movements tenfold.

People's lifestyles duly reflected the economic integration of the empire's provinces. According to US historian Lionel Casson, "The Roman citizen ate bread made of North African or Egyptian wheat and fish caught and dried near Gibraltar. He cooked with North African olive oil in cauldrons made of copper extracted from Spanish mines, used dishes baked in Gaulish ovens, drank Hispanic or Gallic wines [...]. The rich Roman wore Millet wool or Egyptian linen; his wife wore Chinese silk and adorned herself with Indian pearls and diamonds, as well as cosmetics from Southern Arabia [...]. His home was made of coloured marble from the Asia Minor quarries; as for his furniture, it was constructed from Indian ebony or teak embellished with African ivory." The similarities with the diverse origins of the products we consume today are striking. The Mediterranean area of the Roman era formed a true "world economy", in historian Fernand Braudel's words.

That said, the Roman Empire's economic integration was not uninterrupted. There were phases of slowed commercial activity, often during political, diplomatic or military crises such as the Punic Wars between Rome and Carthage in the 3rd and 2nd centuries BC. Several periods of upturn and downturn in economic integration succeeded each other until the fall of Rome in 476 BC, which had a deep and lasting impact on European trade.

The Middle Ages: European downturn, Asian dynamism

Contrary to popular belief, globalisation did not specifically originate in Europe – Asia, the Middle East and Africa largely contributed to its history. To the West, the Roman Empire's division into two entities marked a clear downturn in trade, which political unification by the Carolingian Empire in the 9th century was unable to restore. In Europe, the feudal era was not hospitable to merchant trade, due to its numerous conflicts, territorial divisions, rigid social relationships and rules such as the church's ban on interest loans.

Meanwhile, to the East, the Byzantine Empire continued to trade heavily between Asia and the Mediterranean. Its capital, Constantinople, took pride of place in the commercial network spanning almost all of Eurasia and North Africa and was the first western stop on the famous Silk Road. This major axis – which in fact comprised an intricate network of roads carrying not only silk, but also precious stones and metals, spices, ivory, and so on – spread all the way to Xi'an, in China.

The Islamic civilisation, which spread beyond the Arab peninsula from the 7th century onward, also furthered the economic interdependence of geographically distant peoples by promoting trade between the Middle East and sub-Saharan Africa. For several centuries, Islam's expansion went hand in hand with the expansion of trade, from the north of Spain all the way to the Philippines.

In the 18th century, new global economic relationships emerged during Eurasia's Mongolian Empire as the Mongols crisscrossed the world on their horses, from the shores of the Pacific and Indian oceans to the Mediterranean and the Adriatic. Here again, this geographic expansion led disparate peoples to intermingle and develop relationships. Marco Polo, the most famous Western merchant-traveller of the era, testifies to this in his famous description of Kublai Khan's empire, the *Book of Marvels*.

As for Europe, it was starting to emerge from its commercial slumber in the 12th century. In France, the county of Champagne was a permanent trading centre for merchants from Flanders, Italy and a good part of Europe from the mid-12th century to the late 13th century. Likewise, in the 13th century, the northern European Hanseatic cities and northern Italian merchant cities (especially the Republic of Venice) spearheaded renewed international trade in Europe. They prefigured the energy of the Renaissance era, which opened new perspectives for commerce.

The new horizons of the Renaissance (15th century-18th century)

The Renaissance saw major technological advances and expanded trade through all the continents, setting a new milestone for globalisation.

The intellectual curiosity that characterises this epoch furthered technological innovation and production methods thanks to a plethora of new products and processes, such as using cotton to make clothes. This, in turn, created new needs and new commercial activities, as well as more modern communication methods. The printing press encouraged the spread of knowledge, which in turn benefited scientific, cultural and commercial interaction. Postal services also progressed; in the early 16th century, Franz von Taxis created a messenger network linking Innsbruck to Brussels in only five days. Rather like the Internet today, the printing press and postal service helped world economies to expand, effectively reducing the barriers of geographical separation.

Developments in transportation also played a part. Ships and fleets grew larger. Europe no longer sailed the oceans alone, but was joined on the trading routes by another commercial power, China. The empire's junks (often sporting vastly superior tonnage) sailed the Asian seas and Indian Ocean all the way to East Africa. Perfected navigation techniques (like the compass and cartography) led to a major turning point, at least from a European perspective – the so-called "Great Discoveries". The adventures of Christopher Columbus and Vasco de Gama (among others) pushed back the horizon and traced oceanic routes, heralding the beginning of globalisation in the full geographic sense of the term.

Born from military conquest and conflicts, the European colonial enterprise also went hand in hand with increased economic movement. The constitution of colonial empires – first the Portuguese and Spanish empires in the 15th and 16th centuries, then the British, French and to a lesser degree Dutch, Swedish and German empires from the 17th century onward – spurred the flow of goods and people across and among continents. Products such as tobacco, the potato and the tomato spread throughout the globe in the span of a few decades. Massive production of minerals, cotton, etc., also fostered a no-less massive recourse to slavery for several centuries. For better and for worse, the colonial enterprise helped bring continents together. But ferocious competition among the major powers curbed this trend to some extent.

Trade – A tool of power

Trade grew considerably worldwide thanks to metropolises and their colonies, but the major powers jealously defended their trading areas by applying protectionist measures, according to the then dominant political economy theory – mercantilism. This doctrine assumed that a nation-state's power depended on its reserves of precious metals. To grow richer, the state – at the heart of the economy – had to develop international trade and increase its exports by exploiting the resources of colonial territories. But the tariff schedule forced certain colonies to trade solely with their ruling kingdom and so the international trading posts on different continents stayed attached to their respective crowns (Spain, Portugal, Netherlands, France, Great Britain, etc.). In the 18th century, Britain was Jamaica's only authorised trading partner. Guadeloupe, a French possession, could only trade with French intermediaries.

In *The Travels of a T-Shirt in the Globalised Economy* (2005), US economist Pietra Rivoli describes how British authorities in the 17th century forced citizens to wear wool garments (very uncomfortable in summer) to protect the local wool industry. As a result of opening new trading posts in India, the British had discovered supple and light Indian cotton. Imports began to reach even remote rural areas, threatening the national wool industry. For several decades, this protectionist measure offered a reprieve, until the technological advances of the Industrial Revolution in the following century spurred a revival.

The Industrial Revolution and the explosion of international trade (late 18th century-1914)

The Industrial Revolution marked a turning point in global economic integration. Indeed, some consider the 19th century as the first real historical phase of globalisation, thanks to the unprecedented growth of global economic integration. Originating in Great Britain in the 18th century, the first Industrial Revolution owes its name to a profusion of technological innovations and new production methods. It marked the emergence of mechanisation (particularly in textile manufacturing), mining (particularly coal extraction) and metallurgy. Other European countries and the United States quickly followed in Britain's footsteps. Production developed and accelerated, new needs emerged and new networks were created all over the world.

The Industrial Revolution saw the emergence of the steam era and new transportation methods. Railroads expanded and ships grew faster. Shipping costs dropped drastically throughout the 19th century (see box) as transcontinental travel times shrank, with

Until the early 19th century, global GDP per capita grew very slowly. Asia and Europe remained shoulder to shoulder for a long time

Between 1000 and 2000, the global population grew 22 times over and global GDP per capita, 300-fold. This is in striking contrast to the first millennium AD, when the global population only grew by one-sixth and the global GDP stagnated.

Between 1000 and 1820, revenue per capita grew barely 50%, even though the world population had quadrupled. In two countries, however – Great Britain and the Netherlands, with strongly outward-facing economies – GDP per capita doubled between 1500 and 1820. Starting in 1820, the world economy grew much faster, with GDP per capita increasing eightfold and world population fivefold.

But GDP per capita isn't the only indicator of prosperity. Life expectancy rose significantly. In 1000, the average life expectancy was 24 years. One-third of all newborns died before their first birthday.

Famines and epidemics wrought havoc. Today, the average life expectancy worldwide is 66 years, but is unevenly distributed. Western Europe, North America, Australia and Japan have experienced faster increases in life expectancy.

In 1820, those geographic areas were twice as rich as the rest of the world, and the gap has been growing ever since. In 1998, the wealth gap ratio between these economies and the rest of the world was 7 to 1; it was 20 to 1 between the United States and Africa. But these differences are not set in stone. During the second half of the 20th century, a number of Asian countries showed that it was possible to catch up. That said, Asia's growth was negatively counterbalanced by economic stagnation or recession in other parts of the world.

the construction of the Suez Canal and (later) the Panama Canal. People and goods moved more freely. In the late 19th century, the Second Industrial Revolution furthered the movement, with the emergence of oil and advances in chemistry and mechanics (such as the invention of the combustion engine).

Some major innovations transformed modes of communication. In 1865, Paul Julius Reuter, founder of the famous eponymous information agency, beat a speed record – 11 days by boat – to warn London of US President Abraham Lincoln's assassination. One year later, the first underwater transatlantic cable came into operation, making information almost instantaneous. Distances became more manageable, which had a major impact on economic activity. Prices were set on a global scale. Traders purchased agricultural and industrial products almost in real time, based on the immediate needs of clients at the other end of the earth. By the end of the 19th century, wheat prices in the United States and Great Britain were aligned.

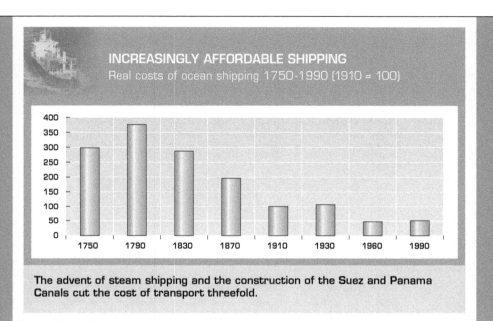

INCREASINGLY AFFORDABLE SHIPPING
Real costs of ocean shipping 1750-1990 (1910 = 100)

The advent of steam shipping and the construction of the Suez and Panama Canals cut the cost of transport threefold.

Source: Crafts, N. and A. Venables (2003), *Globalization in History: A Geographical Perspective*, University of Chicago Press, p. 8, *www.nber.org/chapters/c9592.pdf*.
StatLink 🔗 http://dx.doi.org/10.1787/888932780019

Governments also played a major role in economic globalisation. New laws facilitated capital movements between countries and across continents, professionalising the financial sector. From 1870 onward, Britain's outward capital flows shot up, with half of British savings invested abroad. Likewise, French, German and Dutch capital crossed the oceans, financing the development of the colonial empires. Legal equivalences, such as in property rights, protected colonial investments.

At the same time, the 19th century supported free trade. In 1846, the British Parliament abolished the Corn Laws, which had protected the great landowners from competition by foreign cereal growers since 1815. Great Britain encouraged international trade. Tariffs on industrial exports to France gradually dropped to 24%. Trade in goods soared among European countries. France signed a series of customs treaties with her neighbours (Belgium, Italy, Spain and Switzerland). In the United States, on the contrary, tariffs still

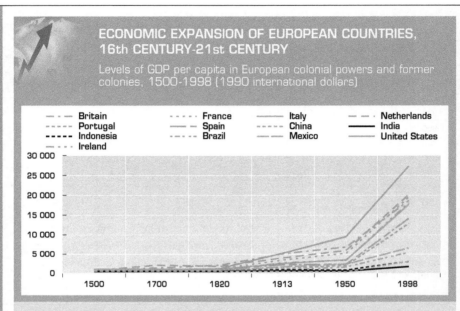

ECONOMIC EXPANSION OF EUROPEAN COUNTRIES, 16th CENTURY-21st CENTURY

Levels of GDP per capita in European colonial powers and former colonies, 1500-1998 (1990 international dollars)

Until the 19th century, European powers were not much richer than their colonies. The gap grew wider as of 1820 and became increasingly pronounced in the 20th century.

Source: Maddison, A. (2001), *The World Economy: A Millennial Perspective*, Development Centre Studies, OECD Publishing, p. 92.

StatLink http://dx.doi.org/10.1787/888932780038

exceeded 45% in 1883. As is still the case today, national legislations and international treaties played a dominant role in the degree of global economic integration. But despite the important rise in global trade, multilateralism was still out of the question. Tariff policies were fixed through bilateral treaties – some agreements were signed at gunpoint. Great Britain in particular, the world's largest economic and military power, dictated her convictions about free trade to her partners and paid very low tariffs to China, the Ottoman Empire and Persia.

Despite occasional protectionist surges, the increased interweaving of economies – whether desired or imposed – remained a major feature of the second half of the 19th century. Between 1840 and 1913, global trade volume grew sevenfold. Between 1800 and 1913, the share of international trade in global GDP rose from 1% to 8%. Alongside these cross-flows of capital and goods, migratory flows escalated spectacularly. During the 19th century, 60 million Europeans emigrated to other continents – an unprecedented movement of people.

The two World Wars
stall the globalisation process (1914-45)

Apart from their very heavy human toll, the two major conflicts of the 20th century dealt a serious blow to international trade. The First World War caused a trade downturn in most Western countries, except the United States. In 1913, exports represented only 3.7% of its GDP, compared with 17.5% in the United Kingdom, 16.1% in Germany and 7.8% in France. As the war drastically curbed European exports, the United States positioned itself as the alternative trade supplier and became one of the largest global exporters of agricultural products.

During the inter-war period, Western countries mostly looked inward. Some historians attribute the rising tension that led to the Second World War to this withdrawal. Following the armistice, national economic networks were still fragile. Countries tried to shelter them from international competition by barricading themselves behind a new arsenal of excise duties. Between 1913 and 1925, Belgium increased tariffs from 9% to 15% and Italy from 18% to 22%. The US plan went one step further, raising the average tariff on manufactured products to 37% by 1925. International trade slowly and briefly began anew in the 1920s until the 1929 stock market crash interrupted the fledgling recovery. Since capital markets were already bound tightly together, Europe was swept up in the turmoil and the globalisation process slowed down even further. In the United States, Washington tightened its trade policy by adopting the 1930 Smoot-Hawley law increasing tariffs on numerous (including agricultural) products (see box). The effects of the law weighed heavily on world trade as the United States' trading partners retaliated by adopting their own protectionist legislation. Between 1929 and 1932, trade expressed in US dollars plummeted 60% and the value of global

The Smoot-Hawley Tariff Act, a protectionist over-reaction	
The 1930 tariff act adopted by the United States has a special place in the annals of economic protectionism. *The Economist* magazine called it the "tragicomic finale to one of the most amazing chapters in world tariff history". Over 1 000 economists shared that viewpoint and wrote to President Herbert Hoover asking him to veto the act. "I almost went down on my knees to beg Herbert Hoover to veto the asinine Smoot-Hawley tariff", recounted Thomas Lamont,	then an associate at J.P. Morgan. "That act intensified nationalism all over the world." Named after its sponsors, the Smoot-Hawley Tariff Act increased about 900 tariffs. Some view it as the major culprit for the catastrophic decrease of international trade from USD 5.3 billion in 1930 to USD 1.8 in 1934. This accusation is probably exaggerated, but the act undoubtedly played a role in prolonging the Great Depression.

exports to USD 12.7 billion – against USD 33 billion three years earlier.

Borders were also closed to people and migratory flows shrank – between 1870 and 1913, the United States welcomed 15.8 million migrants and Canada 861 000. That number dropped two-thirds between 1914 and 1949 – although it's true that improved living conditions in Europe had also reduced the temptation to emigrate.

International trade took off again with difficulty in the 1930s. It only regained half of the lost ground by the eve of the Second World War in 1938, which destroyed the fragile recovery. The collapse of foreign investment is a measure of the impact of two world conflicts on economic integration. Before the First World War, total assets held around the world by foreign investors represented 17.5% of global GDP. By 1945, they represented only 4.5%.

During the first half of the 20th century, countries willingly or unwillingly placed obstacles in the way of globalisation, and yet the protectionist policies of the interwar period produced the exact opposite of the desired results. On the contrary, the second half of the 20th century benefited from renewed multilateralism, which went hand in hand with a rise of multinational enterprises (MNEs).

Find out more

FROM OECD...

The World Economy: A Millennial Perspective (2001): In this seminal work, Angus Maddison presents a complete panorama of world growth and demography since 1000. The author sets out several objectives: evaluate nations' economic performance in the very long term, identify factors of success in rich countries and explore obstacles encountered elsewhere. It also delivers an uncompromising analysis of the interactions between rich countries and others.

The World Economy: Historical Statistics (2003): Also by Angus Maddison, this work comprises the most complete database to date of comparative and quantitative national analyses in the 19th and 20th centuries. It interprets the driving factors at play during different development phases and provides a detailed commentary on the analytical tools that help explain variations in growth rates and income levels.

... AND OTHER SOURCES

On the Internet

Yale Global Online Magazine: This online magazine is the flagship publication of the Yale Center for the Study of Globalization. It explores the multiple (including historical) aspects of global interconnectedness based on numerous studies by Yale University and other academic institutions, as well as the research and opinions of specialists from the public and private sectors around the world. *www.yaleglobal.yale.edu.*

Publications

Bound together: How Traders, Preachers, Adventurers and Warriors Shaped Globalization (2007): In this very lively book, Nayan Chanda, publications director at the Yale Center for the Study of Globalization, recounts globalisation through the saga of merchants, missionaries, adventurers and warriors. Chanda also describes the economic and technological forces at play in contemporary globalisation and offers a stimulating discussion on the best way to approach an increasingly integrated world.

Globalization in Historical Perspective (2003): This series of essays edited by Michael D. Bordo, Alan M. Taylor and Jeffrey G. Williamson offers an analysis of globalisation over time and in various sectors. The first series of analyses shows how the globalisation process can be measured in terms of the long-term integration of different markets (goods and raw materials, work and capital) from the 16th century to the present. The second series examines the importance of technology and geography, the impact of globalisation on inequalities and social justice, and the role of political institutions. The last group of analyses covers the major impact of international financial systems on globalisation, particularly since the financial system became globalised in the 19th century.

Material Civilisation, Economy and Capitalism (1979): The three volumes of this famous work by French historian Fernand Braudel present an economic, social and cultural history of capitalism before the Industrial Revolution. Braudel provides a longitudinal analysis and develops the notion of "world economy", which he distinguishes from the global economy as designating a world region that forms a coherent economic ensemble organised around a dominant urban axis.

3

Despite rivalries between ideological blocs, international trade recovered spectacularly in the post-war era. Western trade liberalisation occurred in a multilateral context which, combined with advances in transportation and communication modes, created an ecosystem favourable to increasingly intertwined economies. This ecosystem allowed companies to develop their activities beyond borders. Multinationals were very important in helping to shape the face of globalisation.

Growing economic integration in a divided world

By way of introduction...

In this month of July 1944 – a usually calm period – the chic Bretton Woods ski station in New Hampshire (United States) is hopping. All the hotels are fully booked. For a full three weeks, their elegant customer base will change the face of the world. The Second World War isn't even over and already, 730 delegates from 44 allied nations are designing the shape of international economic relations for the next several decades.

On 22 July, the "free world" governments signed a series of agreements that introduced a new monetary system, created institutions for economic reconstruction and regulation, and set the bases of a management system for international trade. In 1945, Henry Morgenthau, President Franklin D. Roosevelt's treasury secretary, summarised the spirit of the Bretton Woods Agreement as follows: "Collective measures to safeguard world populations from threats to peace [...] must not rest solely on an international system that manages disputes and prevents aggressions, but also on economic co-operation among nations aiming to prevent and eliminate social and economic maladjustments." This desire for increased economic co-operation heralded a period of intensified globalisation.

From the post-war period to the 1990s, the logic of the Cold War and decolonisation – and particularly the Non-Aligned Movement of countries – fostered world fragmentation. Governments experimented with several political and economic models within their own borders or areas of influence. Even though globalisation progressed unevenly, economic ties grew tighter inside these areas.

The reconstruction heralded an unprecedented era of prosperity, particularly in Western countries and Japan. Between 1950 and 1973, the world economy expanded on average 3.9% annually. The birth rate soared. Sanitary conditions improved considerably. In 25 years, the world's population grew by close to 1.5 billion people. Strong economic growth made it mostly possible to meet this new demand.

An ecosystem that promoted trade took root under the combined effects of the Bretton Woods framework and technological progress. This environment facilitated global economic integration, of which MNEs were a vital driver.

A new global ecosystem favourable to trade

Technological advances played a major role at the end of the war, as is the case at every stage of intensive globalisation. Improved transportation and communication techniques opened up a wealth of opportunities for new economic models.

To begin with, the development of commercial civil aviation brought operators closer together. The first air freight companies were founded in 1948. The jet plane considerably sped up travel. The tourism industry, both for business and private travel, took off. In 1945, 9 million passengers travelled on commercial flights. By 1948, they were 24 million. This number has not stopped growing.

Productivity also grew in the merchant marine. Lower transportation costs arising from the "containerisation" technique in use from the early 1960s onward allowed shipping firms more organisational flexibility (see Jan Blomme's personal view in Chapter 4). The containers protected merchandise better – thus lowering insurance costs – and allowed for faster loading and major savings in handling, stocking and packaging.

The post-war decades also saw a democratisation of the telephone as the main mode of communication. Throughout the second half of the 20th century, the price of international telephone calls dropped significantly (see graph). In 1930, a three-minute telephone call between New York and London cost USD 250. In the 2000s, it is less than 23 cents. The telephone took pride of place in most households and companies in the OECD area. Businessmen and women conducted negotiations in just a few hours and became the kingpins of globalisation.

Political developments also had a considerable impact on globalisation. The Bretton Woods Agreement led to the creation of the World Bank, whose initial role was to facilitate reconstruction and development, and the International Monetary Fund (IMF), whose mission is to guarantee a stable international monetary system – an essential condition of dynamic international trade. The diplomats present at Bretton Woods also considered creating an international organisation specifically devoted to international trade. But without sufficient political consensus to create it, a limited number of countries committed to a multilateral agreement – the GATT (General Agreement on Tariffs

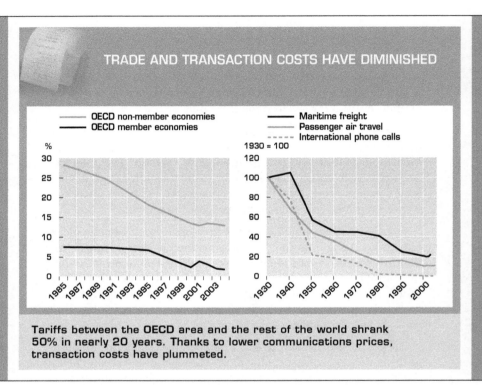

Tariffs between the OECD area and the rest of the world shrank 50% in nearly 20 years. Thanks to lower communications prices, transaction costs have plummeted.

Source: OECD (2007), *OECD Economic Outlook*, Vol. 2007/1, OECD Publishing.
StatLink http://dx.doi.org/10.1787/888932780057

and Trade). The political innovations of Bretton Woods set the foundation for present-day international economic relations and helped shape the face of modern-day globalisation.

Borders open to trade: The GATT-WTO dynamic

The post-war period marked a rejection of protectionism in Western countries. The goal of Bretton Woods was to try, inasmuch as possible, to avoid strangling trade, as occurred in the 1930s with disastrous effects on world prosperity and stability. Signed in 1947 by 23 states, the GATT essentially aimed to liberalise trade in goods. The measures, adopted over several years of negotiation rounds, eliminated a range of customs duties and state-imposed obstacles to trade.

The GATT dynamic had its ups and downs. While many states gradually respected the agreement, some protectionist phases also occurred, particularly in the textile and automotive industries: the 1963 long-term cotton agreements and 1974 multi-fibre agreements aiming to protect industrialised countries' textile industries departed from the non-discrimination rules of the GATT. The multi-fibre agreement was only (partially) repealed as late as 2005.

In the 1970s, the US government threatened restrictive economic measures against Japanese automobiles. Tokyo, which until then had put strict limits on imports, agreed to reduce its automobile exports. In 1977, the two countries signed a bilateral agreement in which Japan committed to limiting its colour television export for three years. Not to be outdone, the European Community adopted restrictive measures in 1983 against a range of Japanese products, from video recorders to vans. At that point, Japanese car manufacturers Toyota, Honda and Nissan decided to open assembly plants in both the United States and Europe, creating numerous jobs. This was not enough to quash tensions completely. In 1987, members of the United States Congress symbolically destroyed Toshiba radio cassette players on the Capitol's steps.

Despite these protectionist episodes, the open-access dynamic of the GATT dominated: between 1947 and 1994, the average tariff level worldwide dropped 80%. In 1995, the creation of the World Trade Organization (WTO), established through the Marrakech Agreement, enshrined this development. The new organisation authorised its member governments to take commercial countermeasures against other members who didn't respect their commitments and created a Dispute Settlement Body (DSB) enabling governments to enforce their rights. But the main objective of the WTO remains pursuing negotiations on trade in goods and extending them to other sectors, such as services and intellectual property. The WTO numbers today over 157 member countries representing over 90% of world trade. By 2008, the average tariffs applied to goods circulating worldwide had dropped to only 5%.

The free movement of capital

Two major events followed each other after the Second World War, transforming the international monetary system and international capital flows. The first came at the end of the Bretton Woods negotiations. For the first time, the 44 signatory countries committed to maintaining fixed exchange rate parities pegged to the dollar and gold (the "gold exchange standard") under the aegis of the IMF. While this new system harmonised monetary relationships, it didn't make all currencies convertible among themselves and therefore was a limited step in global monetary integration. Countries still had strict control over capital movements, which seriously restricted international investment.

Things changed in the early 1970s, with the establishment of a new international monetary system still in effect today. When monetary imbalances threatened the US economy in 1971, President Nixon cancelled the dollar's direct convertibility to gold. In 1976, the Jamaica agreements ratified the passage to a generalised floating exchange rate. All currencies were convertible with each other at a variable rate based on offer and demand. This change isn't in itself synonymous with increased globalisation, because companies now faced a transactional currency risk and national monetary policies could penalise partner countries. But by increasing opportunities for international trade without the need to resort exclusively to gold or the dollar, the new system had a more "globalising" intent than the previous one.

This said, the real novelty accelerating economic globalisation in the 1970s was the progressive opening of borders to capital flows. In 1974, the United States did away with inward and outward capital flow controls. The United Kingdom followed suit in 1979, followed by Western Europe, Scandinavia and Japan in the late 1980s. The European Monetary System (EMS) established in the late 1970s finally spurred the lifting of any and all restrictions to capital movements in member countries. This widespread liberalisation of capital movement fuelled two major components of globalisation: foreign direct investment (FDI) and the internationalisation of financial markets. Both continued to grow in the following decades and played an increasingly vital role in financing the world economy (see Chapters 4 and 8).

In the late 1980s, this movement spread to developing countries. Operating within the framework of the "Washington Consensus", the IMF and World Bank pushed them to adopt structural reform programmes – including opening their borders to foreign capital – in exchange for granting them loans. Initially intended for Latin American governments struggling with serious debt and a public deficit crisis, the Washington Consensus advocates budgetary rigour and economic privatisation in addition to free capital movement. Its principles were subsequently applied to other developing countries. This controversial process – in terms of its economic and social impact – contributed to increasing capital flows among continents.

The developments resulting from the Bretton Woods Agreement, then, profoundly changed the face of globalisation, by establishing frameworks guaranteeing the market economy and free trade, while allowing companies to develop their activities across borders. This institutional dynamic also occurred at the regional level, with a reduced impact on global economic integration.

Do regional economic organisations drive or hinder globalisation?

Several regional economic organisations were created from the end of the Second World War to the 1990s: the European Economic Community (EEC) in 1957, the Association of Southeast Asian Nations (ASEAN) in 1967, the Economic Community of West African States (ECOWAS) in 1975, the Common Market of the South (MERCOSUR) in Latin America in 1991, and the North American Free Trade Agreement (NAFTA) in 1994. All aim to facilitate trade among their member countries and strengthen economic and trade co-operation.

These interest groups, designed to counterbalance the weight of their member states' common competitors, can be seen as obstacles to true global integration. In the 1950s, the regional organisations did not escape the Cold War logic. The Organisation for European Economic Co-operation (OEEC) – the ancestor of the OECD – was founded in 1948 to manage the implementation of the Marshall Plan and facilitate free trade among European economies. In retaliation, the Council for Mutual Economic Assistance (COMECON) – a privileged trading community for Communist Bloc countries led by the Soviet Union – was created in 1949. In its early days, ASEAN also aimed to bring together the non-communist countries of Southeast Asia. Thus these regional organisations reflected the world's ideological divisions.

They also created distortions in international economic relations by introducing privileged relations among specific countries, to the exclusion of all others. The fact that a regional organisation (like the European Union and ASEAN in the framework of the WTO) defends its members' interests in international trade negotiations may contravene the non-discrimination principle, according to which countries must open their trade borders indiscriminately to all other nations.

However, regional organisations can also be seen as embryos – or rather, vanguards – of globalisation. The geographic and cultural proximity of their member countries means that they are easier to implement and that they promote economic integration more effectively than universal institutional projects. This idea appears in substance in the articles of the WTO.

That said, regional economic organisations can vary quite significantly in the degree of economic integration they allow and fall into three major categories:

▶ Free trade zones are a relatively limited incarnation of economic integration. They reduce or eliminate certain customs barriers among member countries, but allow them to maintain their trade policies towards third countries. Examples of this are: ASEAN (a consortium of 10 Asian countries), NAFTA (linking the United States, Canada and Mexico) and ECOWAS (a regional group of 16 West African countries), albeit with mixed results to date.

▶ Customs unions go one step further. They pool member countries' foreign trade policies within a common customs regime. Created in 1957, the EEC is one such union, as is MERCOSUR (grouping Brazil, Argentina, Paraguay, Uruguay and Venezuela), created in 1991.

▶ Finally, economic unions or common markets bring together countries that harmonise their economic and fiscal policies. Goods, capital and people move freely throughout the area and are ruled by the same laws. In 1992, the Maastricht Treaty created a European economic and monetary union that paved the way for the adoption of the euro in 1999. Today, the European Union is one of the most advanced forms of regional economic integration.

As we've seen, a plethora of institutional structures aiming to facilitate international trade and economic integration mushroomed after the Second World War. Entrepreneurial capitalism was also encouraged, at least in the Western world. MNEs took advantage of this movement – and of technological progress – to spearhead globalisation.

The major role of MNEs

MNEs sometimes have a negative image. Some believe they exploit resources at the expense of local populations and the environment and wield a financial power that is beyond the authority and grasp of political power. While the behaviour of some companies may explain this negative image, it only partly reflects reality. MNEs are also important vectors of growth and economic activity and create employment, stimulate innovation and technology transfers. The goal of this chapter, however, is not to evaluate the impact of MNEs on the economy and society – this will be addressed (along with other effects of globalisation) in following chapters – but to describe how they have shaped the face of globalisation.

By definition, MNEs are particularly representative of globalised economic activity because they operate in several countries. By virtue of their economic weight, but also of their cross-border production, distribution and management modes, they are the nerve centres of globalisation. Since the 1960s, they have increasingly optimised their activities by identifying individual countries' comparative advantages at each stage of production and marketing. This has led to unprecedented economic integration.

The quest for raw materials and the convergence of distribution markets

The Dutch East India Company is often considered the first MNE in history. Founded in 1602, it dominated maritime trade for several decades, heading colonies and trading posts in Indonesia, India, China, Japan and Arabia and acquiring such financial might that it minted its own currency. But transnational firms really took off in the late 19th century, thanks to the technological advances and new needs arising from the First and Second Industrial Revolutions and the parallel development of capitalist production methods. From 1890 onward, Standard Oil, the US petroleum giant founded by John D. Rockefeller, started expanding to a number of countries to exploit their precious oil reserves. The first European MNEs were also created at the same time. In 1913, the Anglo-Dutch group Royal Dutch Shell oversaw an oil empire spreading from Indonesia to Mexico.

While the main reason that MNEs set up shop in other countries was to exploit raw materials and strategic natural resources (as was the case of the Dutch East India Company with spices), they also needed to get closer to the products' distribution markets. The import quotas, high tariffs and transportation costs prompted companies to set up local production sites and source their products locally. As early as 1907, French tyre manufacturer Michelin established a plant in Turin in Italy. In 1914, US skin care manufacturer Colgate opened its first foreign subsidiary in Canada. By 1926, Coca-Cola was already present in 26 (mostly European) countries. Meanwhile, several European firms established plants in the United States starting in the 1920s.

The fragmentation of production and quest for low-wage countries

Even though their organisational and management models varied considerably, MNEs contributed to – and sometimes heralded – all the major evolutions of the industrial era. In the first half of the 20th century, product standardisation was the order of the day in industry. In 1908, Henry Ford famously said about his newly launched Model T: "Any customer can have a car painted any colour that he wants so long as it's black." The productivist economy of the post-war boom (1945-75) continued to rely on standardised mass production. This model, which stipulates that demand follows production, held up for over 60 years. It then shifted to a consumption-based model, which paid more attention to clients' wishes. Thanks to their higher purchasing power, consumers demanded more diverse and custom-made products instead of single models. Companies were forced to adapt. The prevailing management model known as Taylorism – a scientific form of management devised by Frederick Winslow Taylor – gave way to more flexibility.

As countries opened their trade borders in the post-war decades, companies faced heightened competition. The growing need to adapt to customer needs and remain competitive generated new management precepts: banish overcapacity and limit stocks, which immobilise capital and raise costs. Companies segmented the production process into modules. The idea of the value chain took over. Production became separated from support activities and assembly work from component manufacturing, thus optimising each stage of the production process to extract new competitive advantages. Networks of external subcontractors (assemblers, producers of components, security, etc.) were organised around major brands, while parent companies focused once again on their core businesses. In the 1970s, International Business Machines Corporation (IBM) and Toyota Motor Corporation were among the first to adopt the value chain model, which became widespread in the ensuing decades.

While this new organisational mode was not limited to MNEs, it did constitute a major turning point that spurred companies to establish operations abroad. As Massachusetts Institute of Technology (MIT) professor Suzanne Berger indicates in *How We Compete: What Companies Around the World Are Doing to Make it in Today's Global Economy,* "Companies, especially MNEs, had reached such levels of efficacy and sophistication that they had to explore new areas to improve productivity and differentiate themselves from the competition. The transfer of certain production units to low-wage countries stemmed from this quest. The economy modularised." (See "Find Out More" at the end of the chapter, as well as the bibliography.) With the fragmentation of production, the reduction of labour costs also became a major parameter. From the 1960s onward, Western companies looked for low-cost labour in countries that were sometimes very distant from their distribution areas. Manufacturing of furniture, textiles, food, cars, electronics, and machine tools was totally or partly transferred to low-wage countries, mostly to the east and south. A new form of international labour division began to emerge.

Hundreds of companies have chosen China as a production site since it opened to the market economy in the late 1970s. Yet the geographic and cultural proximity of firms to their customer base also plays a large role in their decision making. In the 1990s, the signing of the EU accession agreements brought Poland, Hungary and Slovakia closer to their Western neighbours. Transposing the European legislative framework into national law lowered relocation costs and gave investors more legal protection. These countries became destinations of choice for European companies, which could then distribute products manufactured at least cost throughout Western Europe. On the other side of the Atlantic, the 1994 signing of NAFTA intended to give Mexico a similar role towards the United States and Canada. Low Mexican wages enabled companies to manufacture low- or medium-value-added products at least cost and then distribute them in the north.

Despite the massive recourse of MNEs to fragmented production and operations in countries with cheap labour, there was no homogeneous model. Each company followed its own path. Some MNEs chose to duplicate integrated production clusters in different regions of the world. Today, US semiconductor manufacturer Intel has manufacturing plants in Ireland, China, Malaysia, Costa Rica, Israel and Viet Nam. In the 1990s, automotive manufacturer Volkswagen set up an integrated plant at Puebla, following European operational models, while still relying on its traditional outsourcers. Other companies chose to scatter their production, research or distribution centres according to each country's competitive advantage. In 1973, US agrofood company Unilever had one soap factory in each European country. Little by little, the group pooled production activities in some countries and distribution activities in others. Today, Unilever only has two production sites in Europe and uses extremely sophisticated distribution channels to transport its soaps to local markets.

The era of networked MNEs

Having externalised many of their activities, MNEs became veritable galaxies comprising numerous more or less specialised companies that were more or less closely related to the parent company. Subcontractors replaced some internal departments. In 1996, IBM was the centre of a constellation of close to 1 000 listed companies. Gap, the US clothing distribution chain, relies on approximately 3 000 plants worldwide to fill its displays.

It isn't rare for outsourcers of MNEs to be MNEs themselves, with their own network of outsourcers. This holds particularly true for Original Equipment Manufacturers (OEMs). Also called all-in-one integrators, these specialised operators are much more than outsourcers. They propose integrated or even complete solutions to MNEs wishing to externalise certain operations. HP or Fujitsu-Siemens, for example, no longer assemble their computers directly. Most European or American consumers are unaware that the leading global computer manufacturers are Taiwanese and are called Compal, Foxconn and Quanta. Not only does Foxconn, which employs 200 000 people globally, manufacture products for third parties, it also develops them – in 2005, it owned 15 000 patents. In the most extreme cases, the sleeping partner only adds its label to the plastic casing. OEM operators have become the indispensable partners of modern-day industrial firms and are key partners of globalisation. They operate in the consumer electronics, automotive and aeronautics sectors. Aircraft constructor Boeing halved the number of its outsourcers worldwide by resorting to integrated OEMs.

Combined with just-in-time production and delivery systems, this operational network – comprising a complete galaxy of inter-connected and co-ordinated stakeholders – enabled companies to achieve phenomenal productivity gains (see box below on Boeing). Yet these developments had negative repercussions in industrialised countries: manufacturing plants in low value-added sectors that didn't adapt to these changes quickly enough lost ground, shut down or reduced production. But productivity gains in other sectors made up for this phenomenon (see Chapters 5 and 6).

Thanks to its optimised global supply chain, assembly time for the Boeing 737 dropped from 45 to 8 days

In 1992, it took 45 days to assemble a Boeing 737. The aircraft constructor re-organised its production system by involving its suppliers in pre-assembling entire modules, following the example of Japanese automotive manufacturers.

The company eliminated travel by bringing the components directly into the hands of workers through a complex delivery system. Sub-contractors located in Japan, Italy or the United Kingdom began to deliver pre-assembled modules, which only needed to be fitted together.

The joint systems established with the suppliers allowed them to manage orders more efficiently. As they were kept informed in real time of needs up and down the chain, they could synchronise with the pace of the client and anticipate future orders, thus shortening delivery times even further. In 2005, the assembly of a Boeing 737 only took eight days.

The aircraft manufacturer went even further with its Boeing 787 Dreamliner, developing a production plan with dozens of suppliers worldwide (Australia, India, Spain, etc.). This time, the global supply chain shortened not only production lead times, but also the time necessary for research and development.

Under the combined effects of technological innovations, a political context promoting trade, and dynamic MNEs, global trade experienced exceptional growth during the second half of the 20th century. Merchandise exports grew 6% annually on average. In 1970, the share of foreign trade in global GDP had climbed back up to 8%, its early 20th century peak. Between 1955 and 1975, the value of world exports grew nine fold, while world production "merely" quadrupled. Despite a slight slowdown in the late post-war period, the contribution of international trade to global GDP grew – a sure sign of the growing integration of world economies, which stepped up even further in the 1990s.

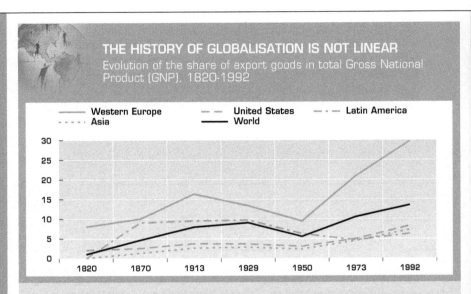

THE HISTORY OF GLOBALISATION IS NOT LINEAR
Evolution of the share of export goods in total Gross National Product (GNP), 1820-1992

World trade contracted after the First World War and only recovered from the 1950s onwards. The GNP share of exported goods reflects the importance of international trade in the economy.

Source: O'Rourke, K. (2002), *200 ans de mondialisation* (200 years of globalisation), *Courrier de la planète*, No. 69.

StatLink ⧉ http://dx.doi.org/10.1787/888932780076

Find out more

FROM OECD...

Staying competitive in the world economy: Moving up the value chain (2007): This report presents a large range of OECD data on the globalisation of value chains and the increase in externalisation and offshoring. It studies the incidence of the globalisation of production in OECD countries at the macroeconomic and sectoral levels and the effect of globalisation on competitiveness in OECD countries. It looks at progression up the value chain in OECD countries and China as research and development gain ground in emerging countries.

The Internationalisation of Production, International Outsourcing and Employment in the OECD (2007): This working document by the OECD's Department of Economic Affairs describes and analyses mass outsourcing, the internationalisation of industrial production and employment in the OECD area.

... AND OTHER SOURCES

How We Compete: What Companies Around the World Are Doing to Make it in Today's Global Economy (2006): Massachusetts Institute of Technology professor Suzanne Berger co-ordinated a vast global study decrypting the workings of modern-day globalisation. Modularisation, containerisation, geographically distributed supply chains... *How We Compete* provides numerous keys to understanding MNE strategies at the core of globalisation today.

Le grand bazar mondial (The Great World Bazaar) (2005): This study by Laurence Benhamou studies in detail how and why consumer goods are produced around the world and are increasingly inexpensive. The book interviews "buyers" who, unknown to the public, seek out least-cost products worldwide. Their testimony as key actors of globalisation allows readers to understand its inner workings.

Smartsourcing: Driving Innovation and Growth Through Outsourcing (2006): Thomas M. Koulopoulos founded the Delphi Group, one of the leading global suppliers of equipment for the automotive industry. In this book, he explains the operation of supply chains and global outsourcing, offering a very pragmatic vision of globalisation.

4

There was an unprecedented integration of world economies
in the 1990s under the combined influence of the opening
of Communist Bloc countries to the market economy and
the ICT revolution. Goods and capital, with a few exceptions,
underwent massive globalisation. Services and workers
experienced more limited globalisation, despite growth
in some areas.

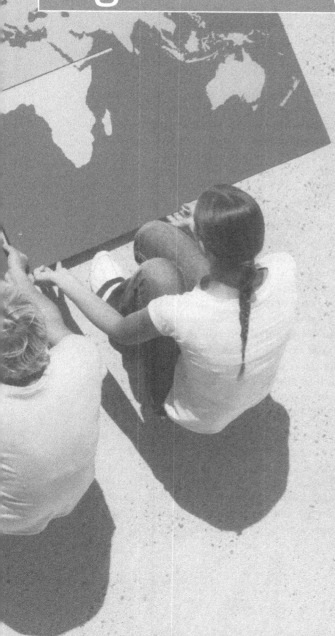

A global or semi-global village?

By way of introduction...

Geneva, July 2008. Following endless days of intense negotiations, the Doha Cycle ends in failure. The World Trade Organization (WTO) members have not reached a compromise on reducing agricultural subsidies and tariffs on industrial and agricultural products. The prospect grows remote for reaching an agreement that places most countries on an equal footing with regard to trade relations – the "fruit at arm's length" mentioned by OECD Secretary-General Angel Gurría. World trade integration remains unbalanced and incomplete.

And yet there has been a major upshift in globalisation since the early 1990s. The fall of the Berlin Wall in 1989 and the end of communist regimes defragmented the world. Western countries continued to open to international trade and pursue the deregulation begun in the post-war period. Hundreds of millions of workers and consumers from the former Communist Bloc countries joined the market economy, followed by a billion Indians, whose country has also emerged from a long period of economic isolation.

The ICT revolution made its mark at the same time. Computer science had become widespread in the 1980s, smoothing the way for considerable progress in corporate management and production methods. The Internet, and particularly broadband in the early 2000s, energised international trade. By creating instantaneous communication, eliminating intermediaries and reducing costs, the Web greatly increased corporate productivity. Made-to-measure component orders, assembly and deliveries were now possible. Companies engaged in direct sales, limiting stocks in favour of just-in-time production and distribution and minimising costs. Client companies and their outsourcer databases also communicate instantaneously. Computer systems now speak the same language, freed from geographical constraints.

For some, this new political and technological paradigm has definitively turned the world into the "global village" predicted by philosopher Marshall McLuhan in the late 1960s: a "flat world" that gives free rein to information and economic flows. For others, there are still many obstacles to trade, despite advances in telecommunications. Some analysts even refer to "semi-globalisation". So which is it? This chapter describes the speeding up of globalisation in the last twenty years and highlights both its intensity and its limits, right up to the recent economic crisis (see the interview with Raed Safadi at the end of this chapter). Further chapters will analyse its impact.

The (almost) flat world of goods and capital

In the 1990s, "globalisation" refers first and foremost to goods and capital. International trade has exploded, due to the emergence of new markets, but also (more surprisingly) to a strong increase in inter-company trade. The financial world is also more globalised and integrated than ever.

A world goods superstore?

Chinese clothing and components, Indian cars, Scandinavian mobile phones and furniture, Starbucks coffee stores in Paris, Wal-Mart supermarkets all over the world, Carrefour in China, Fnac in Rio... This is globalisation as reflected in our daily lives. These familiar brands and products illustrate an underlying trend that has grown in the past 20 years, despite a brutal setback in the wake of the 2007-08 financial crisis.

The trend in the global volume of trade in goods speaks for itself. According to the WTO, that volume grew 3% between 2000 and 2006, then 6.5% in 2007 alone. While the global crisis caused a savage 12% drop in 2009, volume quickly picked up again, rising 14% in 2010. The wealth generated by international trade represents an ever-growing share of total global wealth. In 2005, international trade represented 50% of global GDP, compared with 38% in 1985. Starting in 2002, it grew much faster than global GDP. In 2010, global exports of goods grew four times faster than the GDP, very clearly reflecting the growing commercial interdependence of world economies.

Some emerging economies opened to trade particularly quickly. Between 1985 and 2005, the share of foreign trade in the Chinese economy climbed from 24% to 69%. China, the third-largest trading power in the world since 2008, has become a major trading partner of OECD countries. Nevertheless, trade in goods is still much larger – both in volume and in value – within the OECD area than between

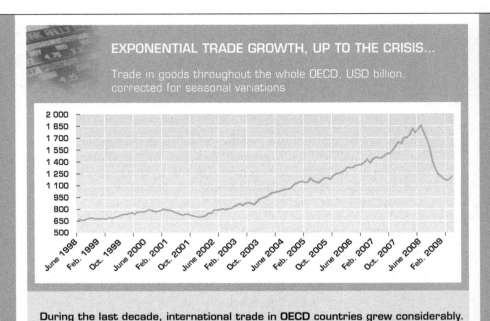

EXPONENTIAL TRADE GROWTH, UP TO THE CRISIS...

Trade in goods throughout the whole OECD, USD billion, corrected for seasonal variations

During the last decade, international trade in OECD countries grew considerably. The 2008 global economic crisis triggered a sudden drop in trade, which resumed at a very fast past pace starting in 2009. In the fourth quarter of 2009, OECD country exports grew by 8%, and imports by close to 7%.

Source: OECD (2010), *OECD Factbook 2010*, OECD Publishing.
StatLink http://dx.doi.org/10.1787/888932780095

the OECD area and the rest of the world. This is due in part to customs tariffs which, while much reduced among developed countries, remain high between developed and developing countries.

The expansion of the European Union from 15 to 27 member countries facilitated economic integration. The share of the 12 new countries in total EU imports rose from 5% in 1993 to 13% in 2005. Some political measures intended to facilitate trade (and described in Chapter 3) seem to have borne fruit.

Intermediate goods, the first driver of trade

One consequence of the fragmentation of production is that economic globalisation today is dominated by the trade and import of components. To produce a finished product – say, a computer – MNE subsidiaries or outsourcers trade its components, for example microprocessors, among themselves. Today, nearly 56% of manufactured goods and about 73% of services exchanged worldwide are intermediate materials and services destined to be included in a finished product or to complete a more complex service. In 30 years, the share of imported components in industrial product manufacturing tripled – from under 10% in 1970 to nearly 30% in 2003.

Low-wage countries have carved out an increasingly larger slice of the cake. Between 1992 and 2004, the share of total intermediate material imports into the OECD area from non-OECD countries rose from 15% to 32%. Today, China and ASEAN countries are the largest suppliers of components of all sorts (automotive, electronic, plastic...) into OECD countries.

"The fragmentation of production constitutes a major phenomenon in the globalisation process. This fragmentation has increased considerably over the last 10 or 15 years at most. Today, numerous countries have found a place somewhere in the global supply chain."

Thomas Hatzichronoglou, Directorate for Science, Technology and Industry, OECD

A consequence of component globalisation is that intra-company trade has exploded as parent companies and foreign subsidiaries import semi-finished goods from other subsidiaries of the same group. Between 2000 and 2007, intra-company exports represented 15% to 50% of exports of foreign company subsidiaries in a number of OECD countries evaluated by the latest OECD economic globalisation indicators.

An incomplete globalisation of goods

Despite the exponential movement of goods around the planet, goods are far from "perfectly globalised". First, a number of obstacles to international trade remain. Thanks to the WTO, tariffs have dropped (to an average of 5% globally in 2008), but some sectors remain highly protected. Agricultural products in particular have been the subject of the new Doha cycle discussions begun in 2001 under the aegis of the WTO. By early 2010, discussions were still stalling between the United States and Europe on one side, and some emerging economies such as India and Brazil on the other. Divergences remain, particularly with regard to reducing subsidies to European and North American farmers. And there are still also a number of non-tariff-related obstacles to trade, in the form of quotas and subsidies.

In real life

Jan Blomme, Strategic director
of the Antwerp port authority
(the second-largest port in Europe)

Jan Blomme has worked for the Antwerp port authority for over 20 years. "We've had to expand the left bank and create new basins to absorb container ship traffic", explains the strategic director, just back from India the day before. "Ports are the thermometers of globalisation."

An explosion of traffic over the last 10 years: "Our expansion in the 1950s and 1960s was mostly due to the development of heavy industry, as well as imports of energy and raw materials. Then de-industrialisation hit Europe, which decreased its coal imports. Automotive manufacturers, for example, diversified their supply sources and reduced their reliance on steel."

Yet the port of Antwerp has never been so successful. Traffic has literally exploded in the past 15 years. In 1990, 102 million tonnes of merchandise transited through the port. In 2007, this went up to 187 million tonnes – "an 80% leap!" exclaims Blomme. All this, thanks to globalisation. "We first saw signs of the stepped-up globalisation process in 1988-90, with the impact of the opening of China to international trade. But the turning point was 1994, when we pulverised our activity forecasts."

"Containers have divided the costs of transport by three": For Blomme,

globalisation is inseparable from the revolution created by container ships.
In 1993, containers represented only one-quarter of traffic in goods transiting through Antwerp port. Today, half of the goods transiting through Antwerp arrive or leave in containers. "Before, dockers loaded and unloaded bags or crates. Containers have made merchandise handling much faster, removing bottlenecks. Logistics flows are much more efficient. To top it off, goods are better protected from theft and accidental damage, which is an important source of savings."

Growing numbers of components and semi-finished products: "The development of container transport, combined with the establishment of new computer and communications infrastructures, allowed companies to manage increasingly complex supply processes", states Blomme. "MNEs have been able to redesign the production process, producing a specific component in a specific area that's either cheaper or better equipped than another. Indonesia and Thailand, for example, have benefited from these movements. Product customisation has also grown. Companies now wait until the last minute for the customer's exact order to assemble the components and deliver the finished product. The distance between the producer and the consumer has shrunk considerably."

In *The Travels of a T-Shirt in the Globalised Economy* (2005), US economist Pietra Rivoli follows the travels of a T-shirt from the cotton field to the store and remarks: "Whatever the positive or negative effects of competitive markets, in my T-shirt's journey around the world it actually encountered very few free markets." Manufacturers and importers taking advantage of tax incentives and subsidised farmers dominate the markets, sometimes forcing developing countries to lower their prices below subsistence levels to remain competitive. The protected goods are often those that would normally give the developing countries a comparative advantage. This trend, however, is on the wane, perhaps because the 2008 economic crisis fuelled fears of a return to protectionism – which didn't happen. A March 2010 joint report by the WTO, the United Nations Conference on Trade and Development (UNCTAD) and the OECD indicated that a majority of G20 member economies had rejected protectionism, considered an obstacle to recovery.

The golden years of financial globalisation

The world economy depends on corporate activity and international trade, but also to a great extent on finance – which has played a major role in economic globalisation, particularly in the last decade. As we've seen, the opening of borders to foreign capital initiated in the 1970s became more pronounced in the late 1980s. This concerns finance in a broader sense – bank loans and commercial credits, stocks and bonds (in other words, portfolio securities), FDI, but also currency exchanges, migrant fund transfers to their country of origin, and so on.

This evolution has had a considerable impact: in 30 years, the value of international financial flows has grown disproportionately compared with that of international trade flows. For example, the value of international banking transactions (consumer loans, business loans, etc.) has exploded, from 6% of global GDP in 1972 to nearly 40% in the late 1990s. Likewise, international transactions on the Foreign exchange market (Forex) have reached dizzying heights, soaring from USD 200 billion a day in 1986 to nearly USD 3 000 billion a day in 2007, according to the Bank for International Settlements (BIS). In total, foreign assets and international commitments in direct and portfolio investments expanded from 20% to 140% of GDP between 1970 and the mid-2000s – a much more significant and rapid evolution than international trade (from about 30% to 50% of global GDP) during the same period. There has, thus, been a major trend towards global financial integration in the past two decades.

But global finance covers a multitude of areas. Here we'll look at FDI, followed by financial markets. The 2008 economic crisis stalled these two essential components of financial globalisation quite brusquely – at least for a while. We'll discuss the resulting soul-searching in Chapter 8.

Widespread cross-border investments

FDI is particularly revealing of global economic integration. When an MNE establishes operations abroad, it can create a new entity or acquire all or part of an existing local company – which includes re-investing the profits of, or granting loans to, its foreign subsidiary. FDI growth often goes hand in hand with growth in international trade of goods and services. As recent MNE strategies have shown, a growing share of FDI is earmarked for developing and exporting foreign production. FDI is thus at the crossroads of financial globalisation and trade globalisation.

The evolution of global FDI is reflected in the surge by MNEs, since the 1970s, to set up foreign operations, particularly in the 1990s-2000s. Global FDI in OECD countries has mushroomed in the last decade, despite a sudden collapse in 2000/01 following the burst of the Internet bubble and the terrorist attacks of 11 September 2001. In 2007, total inward and outward FDI flows in the OECD area were close to USD 3 500 billion – a historic record (see graph). While the 2008 crisis caused a severe fall of FDI in the following year, recent figures indicate a recovery.

Even more revealing of global economic integration is the fact that the share of FDI in capital formation has grown. In the early 2000s, OECD countries spent over 10% of their capital on FDI – up from a 4% average in previous decades. From 2005-08, the relative weight of foreign subsidiaries in industrial sector turnover grew in almost all OECD countries. However, this increased globalisation of corporate financing varies according to the development level of the major world regions.

The dynamism of developing countries with regard to FDI

Until recently, developed countries absorbed most global FDI. According to UNCTAD, developed countries captured USD 1 250 billion in

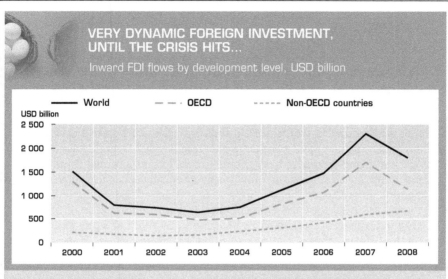

VERY DYNAMIC FOREIGN INVESTMENT, UNTIL THE CRISIS HITS...

Inward FDI flows by development level, USD billion

After a decade of rapid increase, inward **FDI** halted suddenly following the financial crisis in several developed countries. In 2008, inward **FDI** dropped 35% in the **OECD** area. On the other hand, non-**OECD** countries – particularly Asia – continued to receive an important flow of **FDI** (+13% over the same period).

Source: OECD (2010), *Indicators of Economic Globalisation.*
StatLink http://dx.doi.org/10.1787/888932780114

FDI in 2007 – or 68% of the USD 1 830 billion global volume. However, its 2011 report indicated that for the first time in 2010, emerging and transition economies absorbed over 50% of global FDI and represented 50% of the top 20 FDI host countries.

Even more significantly, developing and transition economies also invest abroad. Their outward FDI flows have greatly increased and today represent 29% of global outward FDI. In 2010, six developing or transition economies ranked among the 20 largest global investors. This illustrates the "wealth shift" of recent years, accelerated by the 2008 economic crisis (see Chapter 5).

Increasingly integrated financial markets

Financial markets are also emblematic of the more recent phase of economic globalisation. Take stocks and bonds. They're the most directly linked to corporate activities, which relied on them heavily for financing from the 1970s onward after adoption of a range of rules promoting their use and trade. Stock ownership has become increasingly important in corporate financing systems, to the expense of business loans. Equities – whether as shares in companies (stocks) or fragments of debt (bonds) – feed corporate activity and can be traded like any other product. In parallel with this development, many countries have lifted barriers to international capital movements – as seen in the previous chapter. This has enabled economic actors (households, companies, and governments) to trade securities on all the major global markets. This combination of the growing weight of stock markets in economic activity and the deregulation of capital is at the root of today's very advanced financial market globalisation.

Some facts and figures

First, the annual amount of international securities trading in developed countries has outgrown their cumulated GDP. In the 1970s, it only represented a minuscule share. This reflects the growing internationalisation of stock markets.

Another illustration of this phenomenon: securities traded on the major world stock markets are increasingly owned by foreign operators. According to French Central Bank governor Christian Noyer, non-residents held 46% of French market capitalisation and slightly over 50% of French government bonds in 2007.

Finally, the indexes of the major global financial centres (Frankfurt, London, New York, Paris, and Tokyo) have fluctuated in almost perfect synchrony since the late 1990s. Before that, indexes could behave very differently. Between 1930 and 1950, the correlation between Wall Street and Paris was even negative: when yields went up on one side of the Atlantic, they went down on the other. The fact that the stock market indicators of major financial centres today change in almost perfect unison demonstrates that stock traders can act almost simultaneously in all the world's financial centres.

The weight of financial markets in economic activity has, then, increased strikingly at the same time as they have internationalised. How do we explain this weight?

Principal causes

Three major trends emerged in the late 1970s, called the "3 Ds": deregulation, disintermediation and decompartmentalisation. We have already mentioned deregulation in the wider sense – the removal or relaxing by governments of barriers to movements of capital. Disintermediation means that companies and households can now secure financing directly on the markets rather than through banks. (This phenomenon – largely due to the development of shareholder capitalism – should however be nuanced, because banks remain vital intermediaries in numerous financial market transactions.) Finally, an important defragmentation movement has helped further facilitate securities trading on financial markets: operators can now navigate the different kinds of financial market (money market, bond market, exchange market, futures markets, etc.) to find financing, investments or hedging instruments and trade all sorts of securities across borders.

It is worth noting that financial products have become even more diverse and internationally mobile with the emergence of derivatives. These complex products were designed to spread and minimise risks linked to conventional securities (stocks, bonds, etc.). Since their appearance in the 1990s, they have become increasingly sophisticated and are now a market in and of themselves. The total value of derivatives traded is much greater than that of stocks and bonds. The spread of the 2008 financial crisis stemmed in part from these kinds of product and their internationalisation (see Chapter 8).

Finally, the growing globalisation of financial markets since the 1990s cannot be dissociated from their growing computerisation, which enabled traders to buy and sell securities instantaneously on all the major stock markets. Some traders carry out last-minute operations on traded securities, sometimes with huge sums at stake. And some stock operations are performed today by computers, without any human intervention whatsoever. This further boosts the movement of capital across the planet and reinforces the international integration of financial markets.

But financial globalisation is still incomplete

It shouldn't be concluded from the above that finance is entirely globalised today. First of all, world finance was more integrated in some (essentially monetary) respects in the late 19th century than it is today. Before the Bretton Woods Agreement, the vast majority of international transactions were paid for – and made simpler – with the gold standard, even if international capital movement was otherwise very limited.

In the same vein, the fixed exchange rate system established at Bretton Woods came closer to a true global monetary system than the current international monetary system. Today, governments – or monetary zones such as the euro zone – can exercise sovereignty on their currency rate.

Also, while cross-border investment has increased dramatically, market participants still appear to prefer domestic investments to international investments: both equity investments in companies and market transactions are more national than international. Cultural proximity, then, is still an important factor in financial decisions.

Finally, let's not forget that while free capital movement became widespread in the 1970s, some governments (such as India, Pakistan, and to some extent China) still greatly restrict financial flows.

Services and workers:
A case of "semi-globalisation"?

Today, the services and employment markets are still primarily domestic, due essentially to the importance of cultural factors in these sectors. In many fields, "Globalisation is still just beginning", noted former OECD Secretary-general David Johnston in the *OECD Observer* in 2005. But services and labour cover a whole range of disparate activities, some of which are highly globalised.

The intense internationalisation
of a small number of services

Goods and services represent, respectively, 80% and 20% of total international trade – a share that has remained stable over the past 30 years. In the OECD area, international trade in services represented on average less than 6% of total GDP from 2005-08, and international trade in goods 22% of GDP. Yet services are the largest sector in developed countries, representing 70% of the total value added of OECD economies – a share which is rising.

Several factors explain why services are less globalised. By virtue of their intangible nature, services are less easy to export than goods – it's simpler (in principle) to export a computer than an after-sales service. Many services (such as the hotel industry, personal services, industrial cleaning firms) require physical proximity and for the supplier and consumer to share the same language and culture, which isn't the case when selling a product.

Further, some services are "protected" because they are deemed strategic to the general interest. Depending on the country, education, health, energy and public transportation are more or less protected from international competition. Yet some public sectors (telecommunications, transport, energy, etc.) have been open to competition – especially within the European Union – since the early 1990s.

Despite this, services have been, overall, more globalised since the 1990s. Thanks to ICT, new "intermediate" services – business services, computer technicians, data management, programming, scientific research and engineering – can now be outsourced. Their recent internationalisation has also been facilitated by the emergence of a qualified labour force in low-wage countries.

India, for example, has captured much of the market for these kinds of service. Indian companies have built such critical mass – a single company might employ 60 000 computer technicians of all levels – that they can handle the most diverse requests coming from industrialised countries. Countries such as the Philippines, Viet Nam and China are also very active. Thus a New York hospital chain now outsources patients' claims processing to Xi'an, in central China, where rental and operational costs are 40% lower than in Beijing. This high technology development cluster now exports all kinds of service activities and symbolises the globalisation of a particularly strategic service centre: research and development (R&D).

"While the internationalisation of R&D isn't entirely new,
the current phase has three distinguishing characteristics:
it's gathering pace, it is spreading to more countries, including
developing countries, and it goes beyond adapting technology
to local conditions. In the 1980s, R&D investments mainly
took place between developed countries through mergers and
acquisitions (M&As), but in the 1990s developing countries
became increasingly attractive locations for R&D
investments."

OECD (2008), *Internationalisation of Business R&D:*
Evidence, Impacts and Implications

Since 1996, R&D investments have grown fastest in China thanks to investments by foreign MNEs. The Xi'an innovation area – which should eventually cover 90 km^2 – features a technology park housing thousands of companies. The Chinese space programme was developed here. Several major MNEs that rely crucially on R&D, including Japan's NEC and Germany's Siemens, now develop some of their products there. Meanwhile, US telecom manufacturer Motorola and database software giant Oracle have established R&D centres in Beijing and the Franco-American Alcatel-Lucent group has an important research centre in Shanghai.

Major groups are now also investing in India and run one or several strategic R&D centres there. Since the early 2000s, US industrial conglomerate General Electric (GE) has operated its largest R&D centre (in terms of researchers and performance) in Bangalore, southern India. MNEs are motivated by proximity to a vast supply of qualified personnel, which they can rely on to handle increased demand.

Highly controlled labour flows

Of all the areas touched by globalisation, labour is the least affected. Today, migrants represent only 3% of world population. There are several reasons for this, including the many uncertainties (mainly due to linguistic and cultural differences) inherent in moving to a foreign country. Many countries also strictly regulate immigration according to the state of their economy, their labour needs, and sometimes their identity crises.

Despite the psychological, cultural and political obstacles, labour globalisation is nevertheless on the rise, with increased migratory flows over the past 20 years. Contrary to popular belief and sometimes exaggerated media coverage of the subject, migrant flows do not go simply from poor countries to affluent countries. Today, migration is distributed according to major development areas: one-third of migrants migrate "south-north", one-third "south-south", and the final third "north-north" (north-south migrations are very limited). But it's true that migration from developing countries to developed countries has increased since the 1960s and that the dynamic has accelerated since the mid-1990s. Thus, in most OECD countries, the share of foreign workers in the active population has grown. According to the World Bank, immigrants account for over 10% of the population of high-income countries.

The 2008 economic crisis seems to have somewhat slowed migration. Workers from developing countries are more reluctant to emigrate to Western countries in the throes of a full-blown crisis, particularly in sectors that were once eager for foreign labour, such as the construction industry in Spain and Ireland. But everything indicates that migration from developing countries to developed countries will continue to rise in coming years. This trend also applies to highly qualified workers.

The globalisation of brain power

Many highly qualified workers are more mobile than others and often work abroad or for foreign companies. While a minority have long migrated from one developed country to another, their south-north flows are more recent. In developing countries – and especially emerging countries – highly qualified workers are increasingly numerous. Many of them therefore choose to move to developed countries, which offer higher wages and more attractive career prospects. This feeds the "brain drain" debate as affluent countries attract those individuals most likely to lead their native country on the path to development.

But businesses in developed countries are also going to the emerging economies where the highly qualified workers live. As we've seen, Western MNEs have set up R&D sectors in China and India. The advent of the knowledge economy – where knowledge and innovation are the most important source of value added – means that highly qualified workers are especially in demand and employers are now tracking high potential on university campuses.

In fact, companies are now engaging in global competition to attract those PhD candidates who will become the best researchers in their respective disciplines. Those governments that will win the brain war will have a huge competitive advantage in the knowledge economy. Some higher education institutions now decentralise operations. In 2004, Britain's Nottingham University created two new Asian campuses in China and Malaysia. A growing number of universities are following suit, which allows them to exchange professors, researchers and future graduates. In 2007, 2.5 million students were enrolled in a university outside their own country. This represents a 59.3% increase (and average 6.9% annual increase) since 2000 and is a much faster phenomenon than growth in the total number of enrolled students. Higher education is fast becoming globalised.

By way of conclusion...

Globalisation of goods and capital has seen unprecedented growth since the early 1990s, but the world is still not "flat". The metaphor of the global village is vastly exaggerated, even with regard to the movement of goods. Many obstacles to trade remain and in some sectors globalisation has barely begun. The 2008 economic crisis seems to have slowed it down temporarily (see the conversation below) and highlighted some imbalances. Having assessed the scale of globalisation in its various guises, we can begin to evaluate its effects.

Globalisation is not necessarily desirable in and of itself. Its impacts can be mixed and are sometimes difficult to measure. While some of its effects are obvious, indirect impacts can play a more important role. The following chapter seeks to take stock of the most controversial aspects of globalisation.

A conversation

Raed Safadi, deputy director, Trade and Agriculture directorate, OECD

"We must make the best possible use of our comparative advantages."

Following the 2008 financial and economic crisis, international trade screeched to a halt. Did the crisis lead to "deglobalisation", as some commentators have stated?

Absolutely not. While the volume of international trade did indeed plummet to 12.5% in 2009, this stemmed from factors such as lower demand, the composition of international trade according to the different product types and the lack of financing opportunities for trade that followed the late 2008 financial crisis. Due to the difficulties they were experiencing, banks tightened their credit conditions. This affected all sectors of the economy, and particularly exports, for several reasons. On the one hand, banks consider international transactions as riskier, by their very nature, than domestic transactions. In times of crisis, banks are even more risk-averse than usual in financing international trade operations. In addition, the financial and economic crisis translated into a general drop in demand, including international trade. One could talk of "deglobalisation" if countries had reacted to the crisis by applying protectionist measures, but this was not the case. The OECD, which constantly called on governments to resist protectionist tendencies, wielded positive influence in this respect. In fact, international trade picked up very quickly from as early as 2009. In the fourth quarter of 2009, OECD area exports and imports grew 8% and 7% respectively.

Yet globalisation undeniably helped the crisis to spread. Doesn't this prove that global economic integration can also be dangerous?

International economic relations are like relationships among people: getting close can be beneficial, but living together can require effort. It means making compromises

and taking risks. When a husband or wife falls ill, the other spouse also runs a higher risk of becoming ill – which doesn't mean that the union isn't desirable. One could be tempted to end the relationship and become self-sufficient, but that would mean losing all the benefits of the relationship.

Aren't there examples of countries that have made lasting progress, while remaining closed to international trade?

No. Countries that have remained isolated from the rest of the world with the belief that they could grow and develop just on the basis of their own economy have failed. Look at the USSR; or at North Korea today, which has no competitive industries. The past two decades have shown that countries – and particularly developing countries – that open to trade and economic integration experience enhanced growth and development. In the 1970s, about two-thirds of South-East Asian countries were poor. Today, thanks to their integration into world markets, most are experiencing spectacular growth. Likewise, China owes its economic success to the fact that it opened to the global economy in the late 1970s.

That said, the successful countries you highlight entered globalisation very gradually and kept some regulations.

We're not saying countries should launch into globalised markets without any protection. Some precautions may be necessary to ensure a safe transition to an open economy. The rules of the WTO precisely aim to correct certain imbalances through preferential regimes and derogations according to national strengths and weaknesses. Now more than ever, consensus is necessary within the multilateral frameworks (among others) of the WTO, the IMF and the OECD.

The real problem lies in unilateral restrictions and regulations, which create important distortions in international trade and serious financial imbalances. We must all work towards maintaining an equilibrium.

A conversation (cont.)

Can't a certain measure of protectionism be legitimate in some cases?

Today, a country that adopts a protectionist attitude shoots itself in the foot. Any country that limits imports of certain products would immediately be subjected to protectionist reactions from other countries importing its own products. Given that international trade consists very largely today of trade in semi-finished products, any country that adopts protectionist measures would go against the interests of its own companies, because it would increase the cost of sourcing semi-finished products from the rest of the world.

Globalisation gives companies, consumers and workers the ability to choose their suppliers, their products, their employers, etc. Governments shouldn't limit this freedom of choice, except when absolutely necessary – such as when there is a need to protect public health or security.

But globalisation doesn't always benefit everyone. Some African farmers, for example, are penalised and sometimes threatened by the opening of their national borders to international competition.

Of course, some adjustments can be painful. It's up to governments, NGOs and international organisations to make sure the transition goes as smoothly as possible. But in the long term, openness is always preferable. It's not advisable to aim for food self-sufficiency when a country's climate, soil or topography make farming difficult. Similarly, a country whose agricultural sector isn't very profitable must try to orient its producers to other sectors. It's best for a country to open its borders to agricultural products from other countries and make the best possible use of its own comparative advantages.

Let me add that not all African farmers have suffered from globalisation – as witnessed by the Kenyan farmers who specialise in cut flowers and have been successfully exporting them around the world for several years.

International trade was one of the first sectors to start to recover as of mid-2009. Do you think it will grow stronger?

That will depend on the determination of governments to promote international trade effectively. I think that trade will have stabilised by the time the Doha Agreement is finally reached. Only then will international trade truly flourish. If countries seize this opportunity while taking measures to help vulnerable populations adapt, this will necessarily benefit growth, progress and well-being.

Find out more

FROM OECD...

On the Internet

International trade statistics: This website measures the intensity of international trade. It provides access to several databases on the trade in goods (broken down by product and partner country) and services (broken down by service type and partner country) and the balance of payments of many countries. It also features numerous analyses of international trade data, as well as methodological recommendations. *www.oecd.org/std/echanges.*

Publications

International Trade: Free, Fair and Open? (2009): This OECD Insights manual maintains that prosperity has rarely – if ever – been reached or maintained without the help of trade. Yet trade alone isn't a sufficient condition for prosperity. Policies on employment, education, health and other sectors are necessary to enhance well-being and overcome the challenges of a globalised economy.

Measuring Globalisation: OECD Economic Globalisation Indicators 2010: (2010, available only in English.) This second edition presents numerous indicators: capital movements, FDI, international trade, the economic activity of MNEs and technological globalisation. This edition also includes indicators of the financial crisis, investments in financial products, the environment, and the emergence of global value chains.

... AND OTHER SOURCES

On the Internet

WTO Statistics Database: This interactive database allows users to determine the profiles of many individual countries, as well as groups of countries, in various sectors: trading structure and measures, tariffs and tariff policies, and the main "infrastructure services" (transport, telecommunications, finance and insurance). *www.stat.wto.org.*

Publications

Redefining Global Strategy: Crossing Borders in a World Where Differences Still Matter: Pankaj Ghemawat, a professor at the Esade business school in Barcelona, develops here an original view of globalisation. He insists on the unfinished aspect of the process, which he terms "semi-globalisation". For him, cultural, regulatory and administrative differences still help maintain very defined national borders.

Global Monitoring with the BIS international banking statistics (2008): Based in Basel, the Bank for International Settlements (BIS) collects and analyses a large quantity of statistical data on global financial flows. These resources establish a particularly enlightening map of global finance.

Reaping the Benefits of Financial Globalization: This document, published by the IMF before the 2008 financial crisis, paints a broad and fairly comprehensive picture of financial globalisation.

5

Globalisation first promoted the development of industrialised
countries, then, in the past 20 years, that of emerging countries.
While some developing countries are following in their footsteps,
others have become marginalised or weakened by opening to
international markets. Extreme global poverty has diminished,
but is still ingrained in certain regions. In many countries,
inequalities have deepened. Globalisation can only promote
development if certain political conditions are combined.

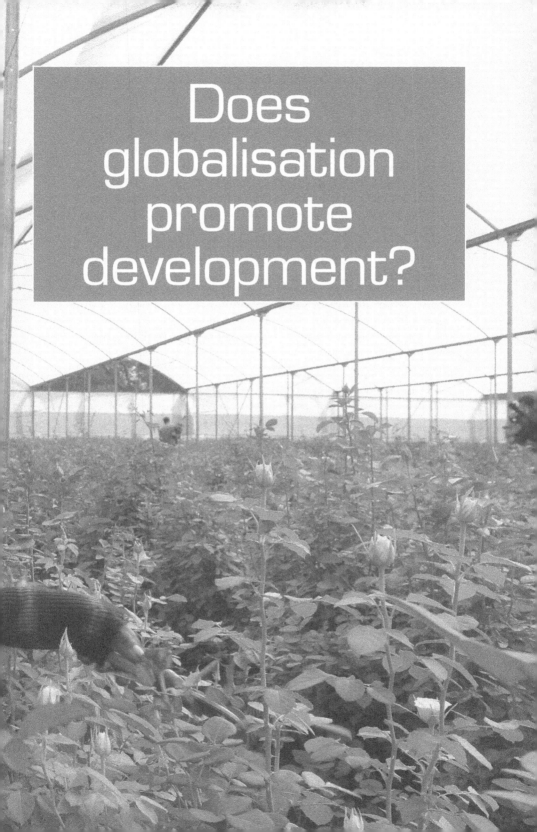

Does globalisation promote development?

By way of introduction…

Twelve years ago, professional manicurist Edmila Silva and her partner Neno left their rural province in northeast Brazil to settle in the suburbs of São Paulo. Thanks to two decades of national economic stability and constant growth, the region experienced a spectacular drop in unemployment over the past 10 years. This success is partly due to the Brazilian economy's integration into international markets: in 20 years, the share of international trade in Brazil's growth has doubled. This led to a range of new jobs and to many families experiencing higher purchasing power. "We have many, many more opportunities than before", says the young manicurist. Today, she drives a small new car, owns a mobile phone and has health insurance. Two years ago, she opened a bank account and took out a consumer loan. She is thinking of going back to school to become a nurse or chiropodist. "I am very independent now", she says. "I have more self-confidence. The future is smiling on us."

At the same moment, in Sikasso, 250 km from Mali's capital Bamako, farmer Yacouba Traoré is complaining about the Malian textile development company – the obligatory intermediary between Malian cotton producers and international markets. "Last year, they paid me 210 CFA francs per kilo of cotton", said this father of six. "This year, only 150 CFA francs." Despite its high quality, Malian cotton can't compete with producers from the north, who supply vast quantities and enjoy high living standards thanks to subsidies. To make things worse, food prices soared this year: imported rice, which is less expensive than local rice, has shot up from 250 to 350 CFA francs in just a few months. "I earn less and less even though the cost of living is higher and higher! Barring a miracle, I'm sure I won't be able to send my two youngest children to school next year."

These are the two faces of globalisation. On the one hand, an opening to trade that brings progress and development. On the other, weakened populations that are trapped in a spiral of poverty. There are two ways to understand the impact of globalisation on development: study the overall situation of countries and study the development of populations inside the countries. Certainly, a country's development level plays a role in the development of its population, but this link isn't automatic. Thanks to globalisation, developing countries are indeed catching up on affluent countries

– but the gulf between the richest and the poorest fringes of the world population seems to have widened.

Globalisation has promoted the development of emerging countries

In the past 20 years, India, China, and Brazil have experienced true economic success stories and progressed very quickly from the status of developing country to that of emerging country. While their key productions are still typical of developing countries, their success is due in great part to their growing integration in international markets.

Asia's economic emergence dates back to the 1960s and the quick rise of the Asian "tigers". From then on, Hong Kong (China), Korea, Chinese Taipei and Singapore positioned themselves as leaders in consumer goods – toys, textiles, mass electronics, etc. The four small territories made the most of their low-cost labour and opened their borders by attracting European, American or Japanese investors. This integration into world markets allowed them to experience a boom. The large emerging countries then followed suit. The political openness of the late 1980s allowed investors from industrialised countries to access almost limitless consumer and labour sources.

The "BRICs" (Brazil, Russia, India, and China) have become a promised land for many foreign investors and industrial companies which were first attracted by the availability of raw materials, then by low-cost labour. As we saw in the previous chapter, production and distribution activities have been shared out among parent companies in developed countries and subsidiaries in emerging countries – principally India and China. The value chain's fragmentation and redistribution to various countries in keeping with their comparative advantages created truly intertwined developed and emerging economies. The centre of gravity of world production shifted. From 1980 to 2000, China's share in the total industrial value-added produced worldwide rose from 1.5% to over 7%. This trend has accelerated in recent years. From 2000 to 2008, China's share more than doubled, reaching 15%. In 2011, China became "the world's factory", a title held by the United States until then.

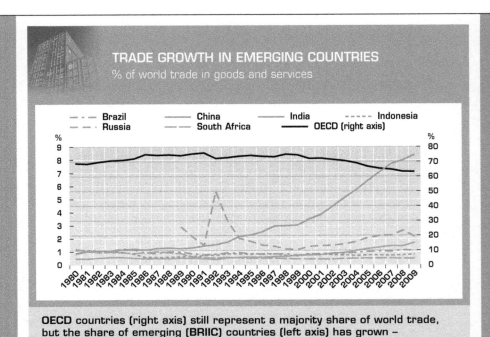

TRADE GROWTH IN EMERGING COUNTRIES
% of world trade in goods and services

OECD countries (right axis) still represent a majority share of world trade, but the share of emerging (BRIIC) countries (left axis) has grown – very quickly in China.

Source: "Globalisation and Emerging Economies", *Policy Brief*, March 2009, OECD, Paris, updated with the latest global development indicators available.
StatLink http://dx.doi.org/10.1787/888932780133

From then on, the Asian giants assumed a growing role in international trade. From 1995 to 2005, the share of Chinese products in total imports to the OECD area increased from 4% to 10%. Trade relations have also improved with developing countries: in 2009, China became the most important trading partner of Brazil, India and South Africa.

This very rapid and intense integration of emerging countries into global markets quickly had positive effects on their economic growth rates, which were considerably higher than the average of OECD countries. China posted growth rates over 10%. Viet Nam, which posted a record 8.7% rate in 2007, now averages 6%. India, Russia, several other Asian countries and some central European countries also post growth rates above 6%, with the result that they have become richer and have accumulated large financial reserves.

Another strong sign of development is that while emerging countries continue to welcome Western investment, they themselves have become international investors. Local entrepreneurs have started businesses in India, China and Brazil. These domestic companies have developed and some have turned to exports, even becoming major world competitors. So, in the late 1990s, MNEs were created in emerging countries. According to the *Global Fortune 500* ranking, their numbers are growing every year. In 2010, 46 Chinese companies (including from Hong Kong, China) featured in this ranking – 9 more than in 2009. India numbered 8 countries – 2 more than in 2005 – and Russia and Brazil 6 and 7 respectively.

In 2006, China became the largest exporter of high-technology goods, although the majority of China's exports continue to be low-tech products while it imports high-value-added goods. A comparison of the trade balance of China's manufactured goods with that of developed countries shows exactly the reverse. Moreover, despite their success, the other emerging economies are still positioned in lower-value-added or primary industries – essentially mining and energy.

That said, emerging countries have recently started to develop in industries where developed countries used to have a monopoly. European and North American companies that delocalise to Asia increasingly do so to access services, high technologies and R&D.

For the time being, the great mining and energy companies (such as CVRD in Brazil and Sinopec in China) do not have much of a footing outside of their national markets. But this situation is also evolving. Companies from emerging countries have begun to diversify their investments. Today, the Chinese oil company CNOOC is prospecting in Africa. In 2008, the international distribution network of the Russian Lukoil group numbered over 6 000 service stations in 24 countries in Europe, Russia and the United States.

Globalisation promotes the "convergence" of new countries

While the growth of the two Asian giants, and more recently of Brazil, has been particularly noticed in the past 20 years, other developing countries have also experienced spectacular growth. According to the IMF, Peru, Nigeria and Thailand posted growth rates in 2010 of 8.8%, 8.4% and 7.8% respectively. The *OECD Perspectives on Global Development 2010* identified some "converging" countries – poor or struggling countries with a GDP growth per capita twice as high as in OECD countries (meaning, 3.75% higher in the 1990s and 3% higher in the 2000s). Their number more than quintupled (from 12 to 65) between 2000 and 2010, while the number of poor countries halved, from 55 to 25 (see maps).

Distinguishing between the role played by globalisation and national factors in this new growth dynamic isn't always easy. But the impact of globalisation on the recent convergence of several countries is apparent in at least two ways: first, these countries have been competing for several years with emerging countries to secure economic relations with developed countries; secondly, they are propelled by their growing trade relations with emerging countries.

Newly attractive countries to "northern" countries

Some countries – in particular Bangladesh, Egypt, Indonesia, Iran, Nigeria, Viet Nam, Pakistan and the Philippines – are experiencing a dynamic comparable to that of the BRICs and could themselves be responsible for world growth in the future. They share dynamic demographics and low wage levels. They have experienced strong growth in recent years, thanks in part to their recent attractiveness to companies from the North. In fact, emerging countries have developed at the same time as labour costs have risen in several world regions. In China, India or Eastern Europe, production costs are rising.

As the case study below shows, these countries must compete with cheaper and more stable economies that stand ready to follow their example and embark on the train of development.

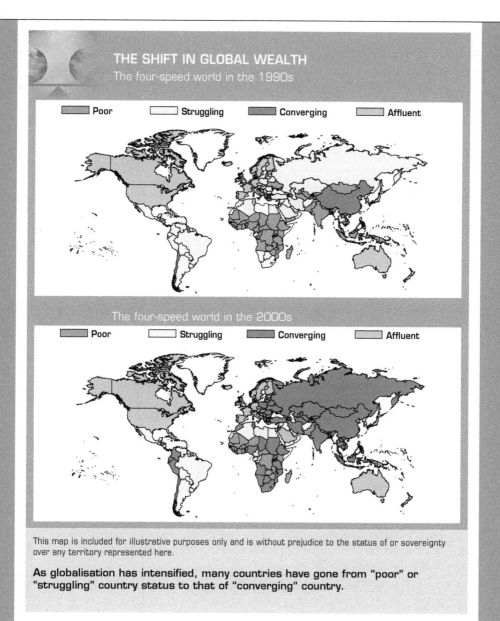

THE SHIFT IN GLOBAL WEALTH
The four-speed world in the 1990s

Poor   Struggling   Converging   Affluent

The four-speed world in the 2000s

Poor   Struggling   Converging   Affluent

This map is included for illustrative purposes only and is without prejudice to the status of or sovereignty over any territory represented here.

As globalisation has intensified, many countries have gone from "poor" or "struggling" country status to that of "converging" country.

Source: OECD (2010), *Perspectives on Global Development*, OECD Publishing, Paris.
StatLink 🐌 *http://dx.doi.org/10.1787/888932780152*

> ### Luggage or toy manufacturing: Slovakia and China are now too expensive
>
> "In 1997, we settled in Slovakia," explains Vladimir Osvalda, former director of US luggage manufacturer Samsonite's Slovakian site, quoted by *The Economist* magazine. "Our other European unit eliminated 100 jobs and we created 100 here in Samorin, on the banks of the Danube. The Slovakian factory was more competitive. This lasted nine years [...]. In 2006, Samsonite closed its 350-employee factory and transferred its production to China. Everything is going faster, much faster."
>
> Economic growth drove salaries upward in Slovakia, making the country less attractive in some sectors with low-value-added potential. Now Central European countries are at risk since cheaper labour is available in the Balkans, the former Soviet Union countries, Africa and Asia.
>
> Salaries have also grown considerably in China's industrialised coastal regions. In the Dongguan area, the average salary grew 25% from 2000-05. Some sectors, such as toy manufacturing, must adapt. In 2005, over 80% of toys imported by the European Union were manufactured in China. But in only 12 months, onsite production costs rose 20% to 30%. In the Guandong province, where most of the toy industry is concentrated, the number of manufacturers plummeted from 10 000 to 2 000 in the span of three years. The cause? Partly the increase in the price of raw materials that followed higher oil prices, but also rising labour costs: in two years, wages rose 20%.

The benefits of "South-South" trade

"Converging" countries probably owe their growth at least in part to their recent attractiveness to northern countries. But developing countries are also growing, thanks to their increasingly important trade relations (whether in terms of exports or investments) with other developing countries.

Between 1990 and 2008, exports between developing countries climbed from USD 0.5 billion to nearly USD 3 billion. Today, they represent close to 20% of global trade (compared with 7.8% in 1990), driven by India and China. While China remains the world's factory, several South-East Asian countries now supply it with components and spare parts. Viet Nam, which experienced close to 8% growth rates in recent years, produces more and more industrial goods for China.

African countries such as Angola, Equatorial Guinea, Nigeria, the Republic of Congo and Sudan are benefiting from China's rising energy requirements. They represent over 80% of oil and raw materials exports to China. South Africa, on the other hand, is responsible for 86% of all African exports to India.

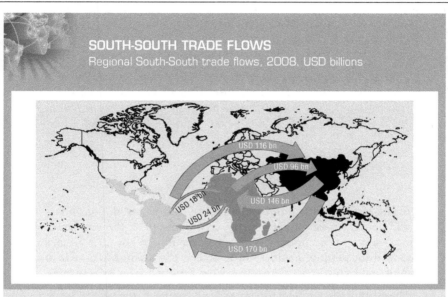

SOUTH-SOUTH TRADE FLOWS
Regional South-South trade flows, 2008, USD billions

USD 116 bn

USD 96 bn

USD 18 bn

USD 24 bn

USD 146 bn

USD 170 bn

Trade between Asian countries, pulled by development in India and China, account for about ¾ of South-South trade. But trade between Asia and Latin American countries is also strong.

Source: OECD (2010), *Perspectives on Global Development*, OECD Publishing, Paris.

Young MNEs from BRIC countries are not lagging in international investments and have invested heavily in developing countries in recent years. Today, the main telecommunications operators in developing countries also come from developing countries. Here, too, China has pride of place and is increasingly positioning itself as a constructor of infrastructure and buildings in (among others) Africa, the Maghreb and Ethiopia. It is also playing a wider role in the mining sector and buying up arable land in several African countries. In 2008, Indian automotive constructor Tata Motors launched the Nano – the "car of the people" – aimed at consumers in developing countries. But it wasn't very successful.

The often indirect link between globalisation and development can be difficult to explain. But there's no doubt that the opening of developing countries (particularly China and India) to international trade has stimulated their economies. It's estimated that 1% additional growth in China generates about 0.2% of growth in poor countries and 0.3% in intermediate countries.

That said, the growing integration of developing countries with northern and southern economies doesn't benefit all countries equally.

Very different dynamics depending on the countries

In the last 20 years, rapid globalisation has occurred alongside a worldwide decrease in extreme poverty. Since 1990, the number of people surviving on under USD 1 a day has dropped by 25% – that's 500 million people. From 1990 to today, the share of the world population living in extreme poverty has dropped from 31% to 19%.

These numbers owe a lot to China's good results. In the past 15 years, China's per capita income grew faster than in most developing countries. In 1981, 835 million Chinese lived on less than USD 1.25 a day, compared with "only" 208 million today. The "world's factory" is going at full capacity – which doesn't necessarily make its neighbours very happy. Not only is poverty not decreasing in other countries and regions around the world, it's sometimes increasing.

In southern Asia, the number of people living in poverty has risen despite the high growth rates experienced by many of the region's countries. India's indigent population has soared to 36 million in the same 15-year period. As a share of total population, though, poverty has actually decreased from 58% to 42%. But while millions of Indians now subsist on more than USD 1.25 a day, 75% still live on less than USD 2 a day.

As for sub-Saharan Africa, it is still lagging behind in terms of development. A full 50% of its population has been living in poverty for the past 30 years. Two-thirds of the poorest people on earth live in Africa. It wasn't always this way. In 1970, 11% of the world's poorest lived in Africa, compared with 76% in Asia. The ratio has completely reversed in under 30 years.

Some world regions have become poorer. Comparatively speaking, the poorest country in 2011 was poorer than the poorest country in 1980. And much of humankind continues to live on less than USD 1 a day.

Globalisation can contribute to instability

Not all the developing countries have benefited from globalisation. Many countries have stagnated in the past 20 years. In 2006, GDP in 42 world countries did not exceed USD 875 per capita. Among these were 34 countries in sub-Saharan Africa (Madagascar, the Republic of Guinea, Democratic Republic of the Congo...), 4 in Latin America (Bolivia, Guyana, Honduras, Nicaragua) and 3 in Asia (Myanmar, Laos, Viet Nam – although the latter just joined the intermediate country classification in 2010). Among the 49 least advanced countries, according to the United Nations definition, were Bangladesh, Yemen and Haiti.

Why have these countries not succeeded in hoisting themselves onto the international economic stage? A number of factors are involved. Geographic and climatic conditions, as well as conflict situations, sometimes nip any possibility of development in the bud. The political context also plays an important role. Of course, most often it's isolationism – as opposed to openness to trade – that's responsible for under-development, as witnessed by North Korea's insistence on self-sufficiency. But openness to trade also creates some weakness. One of the main drawbacks of globalisation is the instability it creates, which manifests itself in several ways:

Dependence on raw materials

Some countries owe their presence on the international economic stage essentially to their raw materials, found in agriculture, mining and oil extraction. Yet the prices of these raw materials are very volatile and dependent on global supply and demand. Countries that export a single raw material, like several African countries or Venezuela (with oil), are at the mercy of a drop in prices. The same goes for ore and agricultural products, such as cotton for Mali. These countries must try to diversify their economy and make sure they have stable sources of revenue.

Exposure to speculative bubbles

While the free movement of capital across borders has certainly oiled economic wheels, it can also be a source of instability. Although it can be beneficial in the short term, it can be devastating in the long term if the capital injected into a country's economy is purely speculative. Investors can sometimes buy massive quantities of shares in listed companies in developing countries at prices that are out of all proportion to the real wealth generated by these companies. The speculative bubbles created like this can burst at the slightest economic shock. The ease with which capital can now move means that money injected into a national economy can leave just as quickly. This is in part the origin of the 1990s financial and economic crises, particularly in South-East Asia and Argentina.

The weakness of local companies faced with international competition

Often, developing countries that open to international trade don't have major national operators. So when foreign MNEs set up in the country, they capture the best part of the market, at the expense of local operators and sometimes entire economic sectors. Foreign giants, whether Western or Asian, secure positions of near-monopoly, maintaining high prices and preventing local companies from developing. National economic operators remain restricted to purely domestic economic sectors. This means that a too brutal opening to international trade and investment can prove risky for countries that lack a well-developed economic fabric. These risks weigh on developing countries' economic and social cohesiveness.

Globalisation contributed to widening inequalities among social groups

According to a 2008 International Labour Organization (ILO) study, income inequality grew in the majority of countries from 1990-2005. This holds true for most developed countries because of their progressive de-industrialisation. Low-skilled workers – who are more numerous than others – have seen their wages wither away. In the next chapter, we will study more closely the widening wage gap in developed countries.

In emerging countries, globalisation has sometimes grown in appearance only, as inequalities grew constantly in the 1980s and 1990s. During that period, Mexico hoisted itself among the 10 most dynamic countries in terms of international trade. Yet it seems less egalitarian today than it was a decade ago: nearly 50% of the population of 109 million lives on less than 400 pesos (about USD 30) a day, while 10% of the population owns the equivalent of 50% of the GDP.

Likewise, inequalities in China deepened in parallel with its frenzied growth from 1990-2005. Since then, income disparities seem to have become smaller and even receded in some Chinese regions (see graph). In India, there is a striking contrast between the "shining India" of Bangalore and the rest of the country. High-tech industries only employ 0.2% of workers, and only 2% of workers participate in globalisation through exports of high-value-added goods. According to the United Nations Development Programme (UNDP), 92% of India's economic activity depends on the informal sector. The rural world is plagued by corruption and bad governance. The winners and losers of globalisation live side by side within one same country. However, in other emerging countries like Brazil and South Africa, inequalities have shrunk in the past two decades (see graph).

The fruits of globalisation are therefore very unevenly distributed. The integration of economies in world markets has a strong impact on wages, by favouring some sectors in the great global competition. So, for example, wage increases mostly concern mobile workers and technology workers. Economic growth reflects less quickly on low-skilled workers and those who remain frozen in a geographic area or sector (that is, if they don't move out of a declining activity towards a growth activity). In large emerging countries, poverty is less prevalent in cities. Chinese peasants who chose to remain in the countryside have not seen their income rise as much in recent years as those who migrated to cities.

Some improvement in living standards

Even though globalisation sometimes increases inequalities, the opening of borders to trade has also gone hand in hand with a global increase in the middle classes. Many people have benefited from the economic dynamism and new jobs that result from international trade. They have also benefited from the quick spread of technologies, competencies and knowledge, with sometimes very positive effects on health. Infant mortality has dropped significantly worldwide and life

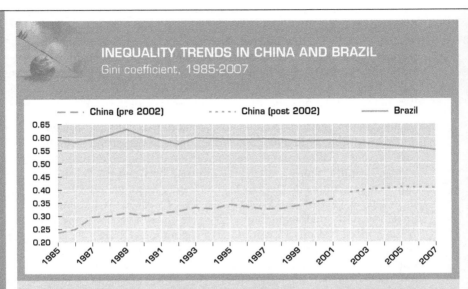

INEQUALITY TRENDS IN CHINA AND BRAZIL
Gini coefficient, 1985-2007

The Gini coefficient is a variable number between 0 and 1, where 0 means
perfect equality (everyone has the same income) and 1 means total inequality
(one person has all the income, others have none). In Brazil, inequality seems
to be shrinking, but its starting level is much higher than in China. China has
seen a marked rise in inequality, with a particularly strong increase between
1990-2005. Its Gini coefficient went from 0.30 to 0.40 during this period,
shifting inequalities in China from a level close to the average level of inequality
in OECD countries (0.30) to the average level of inequality in OECD countries
where it is highest. Since 2005, however, the inequality level seems to have
stabilised.

Source: OECD (2010), *Perspectives on Global Development*, OECD Publishing, Paris,
*www.oecd-ilibrary.org/development/perspectives-on-global-development-
2010/inequality-in-selected-countries-1985-2007_9789264084728-graph46-en.*
StatLink ⟐⟐ *http://dx.doi.org/10.1787/888932780171*

expectancy in developing countries is today around 65 years – still
10 years less than in developed countries. Literacy rates have risen by
over 10% since the 1970s, which in turn has reinforced the interconnectedness of developing countries with the rest of the world economy.

From a political standpoint, economic growth and openness to
trade have also encouraged a demand for democracy and represen-
tation. Today, most of the world population lives in countries run by

elected governments. The number of countries that have adopted civil and political rights and freedom has grown.

By way of conclusion...

The overall picture is mixed. As in developed countries, globalisation stimulates progress in developing countries, by improving the allocation of resources, thanks to greater comparative advantages, decreased costs due to economies of scale, and higher dynamism through technology transfers.

In 2007, a Pew Research Center poll of "ordinary citizens" in 47 countries showed that most believed the increase in international trade had a positive impact on their country – an opinion that was particularly widespread in the poorest countries and especially in sub-Saharan Africa. Eighty per cent of respondents in the 10 African countries polled viewed international trade as beneficial.

But the mutations caused by globalisation also make the weaknesses of certain countries and population categories more apparent. Globalisation creates instability because it forces the weakest companies to compete with the best-armed companies, places some populations at the mercy of global prices and marginalises some economic sectors. However, a country's development level is only partly reliant on globalisation (see the conversation below with Andrew Mold).

In summary, while globalisation is necessary to development, it doesn't necessarily guarantee that development and can even be risky. Only a range of well-considered policies – both economic and social – can help countries reap its full benefits. Let's review a few examples.

First, as stated above, developing countries must rid themselves of their dependence on raw materials and diversify their economies. Not only is the raw materials sector volatile, it also doesn't generally benefit other economic sectors. Therefore, governments must take advantage of periods of high raw material prices to combat poverty and inequality and diversify by developing industry and services.

Further, countries must make the most of their domestic market. No one develops sustainably by opening to international trade from one day to the next. Countries that open to trade without having laid out a strong domestic economic foundation don't generally perform well in the long term.

Likewise, developing countries need to co-operate more with their neighbours. Even if some economists see regional integration as distorting international trade, it does seem to act as a stepping stone to the world economy. It offers a means for small countries in particular to gain confidence and make the most of their competitive advantages.

Finally, innovation, education and training are crucial to making the most of globalisation. While this may seem obvious, many countries are still lagging behind in this respect. The only way to develop is to acquire technology and knowledge of the most efficient production modes. South-South co-operation could still grow considerably in this area.

A conversation

Andrew Mold, former Head
of Competitiveness and Structural Analysis
Unit, OECD Development Centre

"Openness to international trade isn't a good thing in itself. What's important is to gain in value-added and above all, to increase the country's technological capacity."

Do you believe globalisation promotes development?

That's a big question! Overall, I would say that a slow and progressive opening to the world economy is beneficial to developing countries. Economically speaking, the market economy and the spread of technologies are vectors of progress. Some recent phenomena, like MNEs adapting their products to the poorest consumers – the "bottom of the pyramid", to borrow a term coined by C.K. Prahalad – also bode well for development.

Nevertheless, other aspects of globalisation are worrisome, like the pressure on the wages of low-skilled workers in some developed countries or issues linked to the environment and sustainability of growth. Resource depletion and environmental conservation are major constraints to growth. The fact that several countries participate in the production

of a single good can lead to greater cost efficiencies, but have a negative impact on the environment. For example, the fact that Zambian farmers produce green peas for British supermarkets or that Ethiopia and Colombia export flowers to the Netherlands is probably a good thing for workers in the sector, but the ensuing air travel is an important source of pollution and CO_2 emissions.

I also share the opinion of authors Peter Gibbon and Stefano Ponte who observe in their book *Trading Down: Africa, Value Chains and the Global Economy* that most African countries are restricted to a limited share of the globalised markets and to certain types of production because a small number of operators control the value chains. Some buyers act as true monopolies in their relationships with agricultural suppliers in developing countries, with the result that there are one or two buyers and thousands of vendors – which doesn't promote proper market functioning.

In brief, while globalisation is rather positive overall, it does pose some important problems, which require global solutions.

A conversation *(cont.)*

Are there no examples of countries that developed without opening to international trade?

The formerly communist Albania and present-day North Korea are examples of quasi-autarkic economies. I don't think you can say these countries are economic success stories! No, a country that is closed in and on itself cannot develop sustainably. But there are many ways to open up. Some countries developed their exports while partially protecting their domestic market. This is what Korea did in the 1960s and 1970s. Mexico, on the other hand, while it managed to increase significantly the volume and diversity of its exports, still has low – indeed, almost stagnant – GPD per capita. How do you explain these differences between the two countries? What's important isn't the volume of trade or FDI, but the type of trade and FDI, as well as the level and effectiveness of legislation. Even though the volume of Mexican imports has grown considerably, their value added owing to *maquiladoras* (factories that make products destined for export from imported components) remains very low – partly because they must pay more for components than their Asian rivals.

Openness to international trade isn't a good thing *in itself.* What's important is to gain in value added, and above all to grow the country's technological capacity. Developing countries must climb the value chain rather than remain confined to producing low-value-added goods. Even China is confronted with this challenge. The Chinese government is pushing MNEs to perform transfers of technology, skills, and so on. But these efforts are partly an illusion because in the end, the effectiveness of technology transfers is mostly in the hands of MNEs, which are not always keen.

The principle of opening borders to trade was long put forward as a condition of development. Yet the countries that have developed the most, like China, have retained some control over international trade,

and particularly capital movements. Should developing countries open to trade or not?

That's a key question. Some recent studies refer to "threshold levels": a single country can't benefit from trade and capital flows if it hasn't established first a minimal level of institutional capacity and human capital. Barring that, opening to trade leads to increased instability arising from the most liberal policies. Many poor countries have experienced this.

Owing in particular to the financial and economic crisis, I think we're moving towards more pragmatic policies. For example, the IMF recently indicated that some forms of control over economic flows could sometimes be beneficial. Developing countries must seek to develop their own policy mix.

Perspectives on Global Development 2010 [updated in 2012] expressed renewed optimism about developing countries as a whole. The report indicates that while the 1990s were a "lost decade" for many of them, the past decade was much more positive. Does globalisation hold any hope for these countries?

Yes, there is hope. Several factors explain the economic progress of developing countries: in the 2000s, the international economic context improved considerably for the developing world, thanks to lower interest rates and abundant global liquidity. Today, developing countries overall have much more prudent macroeconomic and budgetary policies. Finally, in the 2000s, international trading terms became much more interesting for developing countries, thanks particularly to the rising price of raw materials – and particularly minerals – fed by the demand of the two Asian giants. Developing countries, as producers of raw materials, had been awaiting these price increases for years.

A conversation *(cont.)*

But this new situation is a double-edged sword. According to the joint report on agriculture from OECD and the Food and Agriculture Organization of the United Nations (FAO), cereal prices should increase another 40% in the next decade. Yet some developing countries are net importers of foodstuffs, and this phenomenon makes their imports more expensive. Consequently, this new context creates opportunities, but also raises great challenges. The rise in basic food prices is already having dire repercussions in some countries.

Overall, globalisation seems to be widening inequalities...

This can happen, but governments should not invoke globalisation to justify widening inequalities. This phenomenon also affects developed countries, as indicated in the 2011 OECD report *Divided We Stand: Why Inequality Keeps Rising*. For example, the growth experienced in the United States right up to the crisis mainly benefited the wealthiest segment – 1% to 5% – of the population. At the same time, the wages of low-skilled workers stagnated (see Chapter 6). Governments can change this paradigm through taxation and social protection: the excessive widening of the inequality gap isn't a "natural" consequence of growth and development.

Find out more

FROM OECD...

On the Internet

OECD Development Centre:
This website provides access to most reports, databases, studies and conferences of the OECD Development Centre, including on the impact of globalisation on development. www.oecd.org/dev.

Publications

Perspectives on Global Development (2010): *Shifting Wealth*, the first volume of this new annual publication series by the OECD Development Centre published in June 2010, examines the impact of the rise of major emerging economies on development, poverty and inequality.

"The Social Impact of Foreign Direct Investment" (2008): This OECD policy brief studies the real social impact of FDI in developing countries, including FDI impact on workers, working conditions in MNEs compared with local firms, the effects of FDI on the overall economy and the means by which governments can ensure that FDI enhances development.

... AND OTHER SOURCES

On the Internet

World Bank "Data and Research" Website: Contains numerous data, information and analyses, including estimates of global and regional poverty rates. http://econ.worldbank.org.

2010 UN report on the Millennium Development Goals: This report periodically evaluates progress towards achieving the MDGs. The 2010 report shows that extreme poverty (the share of people living on less than USD 1.25 a day) dropped in most world regions during the 1990s. The 2008 crisis, however, triggered a surge in extreme poverty (see www.un.org//millenniumgoals/report2010.shtml).

Publications

World Bank Global Economic Prospects: One of the most exhaustive analytical tools available to policy makers, this takes stock of the state of economic development in developing countries.

The Fortune at the Bottom of the Pyramid (1st edition, 2004): Economist C.K. Prahalad explains how economic development could reach the shores of developing countries if MNEs considered consumers from poor southern countries as fully-fledged consumers and enacted a commercial strategy adapted to their needs and purchasing power. This would open a market of 4 billion potential consumers.

In Defense of Globalization (1st edition, 2004): Professor Jagdish Bhagwati of Columbia University noted the numerous critiques of globalisation over the past 20 years and answered each of them, insisting on matters of economic development.

6

Even though competition from low-wage countries has some
negative effects on employment in OECD countries, the link
between globalisation and job losses is less obvious than it first
appears. In times of economic shock such as the recent
recession, globalisation seems to create more jobs overall than it
destroys. Likewise, the total increase in wage inequality of the
past two decades seems more linked to technology and
legislation than globalisation – which does nevertheless
undeniably contribute to increased job insecurity in some cases.
The challenge is to help the "losers" of globalisation stay in the
race and seize the new opportunities offered by openness to
international trade.

Does
globalisation
promote
employment?

By way of introduction......

In January 2008, mobile phone manufacturer Nokia announces it's closing its factory in Bochum (Germany), moving production to Cluj-Napoca (Romania) and axing 2 300 jobs. One year earlier, Ben-Q/Siemens and Motorola also closed their German production sites. And yet the mobile telephone market, born only 15 years earlier, is still young. Faced with the emotion triggered by this announcement, the German government demands that Nokia reimburse the EUR 17 million it received in subsidies.

International competition has grown in most sectors. Companies want to reduce costs. For many years, offshoring has been a means to this end. The gradual diversification and internationalisation of share-holders has reduced many companies' local foothold, creating uncertainty and worrying workers in developed countries, whose jobs constantly risk being transferred to the other side of the globe.

This uncertainty has been prevalent for decades, and the 2008 crisis, with its devastating effects on jobs, has increased it. In many countries, the employment situation has got considerably worse. Economies previously characterised by relatively low unemployment rates have seen them soar. Between December 2007 and March 2010, jobless rates rose from about 4.5% to slightly over 8% in the United Kingdom. The rise in unemployment has been even more acute in the United States, with rates climbing from 4.5% to close to 10% of the workforce.

This chapter looks at the impact of globalisation on employment in the past 20 years. This is no easy feat. As we've seen, globalisation involves different phenomena, from international trade through migration to FDI. Some clues can help us evaluate the impact of globalisation on employment, but they can also mask the less visible underlying trends, both in terms of employment *volume* and job *quality*.

Globalisation destroys some jobs, but creates many more

Offshoring, while certainly painful, is only one aspect of globalisation. An analysis of the global effects of the increased economic integration of different world regions reveals a complex reality. Here, we mostly concentrate on employment tendencies in OECD countries because unemployment has been widespread since the late post-war period and here more than elsewhere, globalisation has been blamed for robbing workers of their jobs. Some employment trends in developing and emerging countries appear in parallel as jobs lost in some sectors in OECD countries often appear as jobs gained in other regions.

Job losses due to competing goods from emerging countries

Imported products competing against domestic products have spawned job losses in OECD countries. The new configuration of international trade discussed in Chapter 4 is characterised by the decreased competitiveness of some goods manufactured in developed countries compared with those from emerging countries.

It is difficult to establish the total volume of job losses due to international competition, because the link between the two is often indirect and not clear-cut. Even so, the evolution of employment data in some industries is telling. Since the 1990s, industrial employment has backtracked in most OECD countries – a symptom of the de-industrialisation of developed countries. In the 1990s, a flood of clothing made in China that was sold at unbeatable prices proved fatal to a vast swathe of the textile industry in several OECD countries. Many companies were forced to downsize or close down. From 1970-2003, the textile workforce dropped 60% in G7 countries. This carnage caused OECD companies to refocus on branches with higher value added, such as textile technology, design, haute couture, etc. Similar trends affected mass electronics, toys, household objects and other sectors whose products did not require specialised skills and technology.

But some industrial activities – such as agribusiness, chemicals (including pharmaceutical products) and cars – remain a source of employment in OECD countries. These sectors maintained a more or less stable workforce over the past 25 years, at least up until the recent economic crisis. In the case of agribusiness, industrial processing must often be located close to the distribution market. This means that international competition has less of an impact on the activity and the way it's organised, so the industry is relatively safe from the strong winds of international competition.

But competition can also be beneficial to workers in developed countries. The automotive, pharmaceutical and chemical sectors are largely dependent on international competition, which has not affected their employment levels. This is because, unlike the textile or mass electronics sectors, they essentially export and import among OECD countries which, as it turns out, manufacture more or less the same type of products. For example, German automobile imports to France don't threaten French automobile production, because France also exports its cars to Germany and other OECD counties. In other words, it's mostly competition among *some* imported goods – lower-value-added goods produced in developing and emerging countries – that causes some job losses in OECD countries.

Not all the OECD countries have evolved in the same way. In Korea, Mexico or Ireland, the number of industrial jobs has risen. Since the industrial fabric developed late, these countries are catching up in effect, thanks in part to foreign investment. In the 1990s, US personal computer manufacturer Dell established a base and created over 4 500 jobs in Ireland. In recent years, most Dell PCs sold in Europe were assembled at Limerick. Thanks to the huge number of computers exported from its Irish base, Dell contributed nearly 5% of the Irish GDP. Yet in 2009, caught up in the global crisis, the company closed its Limerick unit and transferred production to Poland.

The North's de-industrialisation and its negative effects on employment are also due to another form of competition – wage competition, which prompts many OECD companies to outsource production.

Loss of jobs due to offshoring

The impact of offshoring in OECD countries can't be overstated. Some of the research is quite worrisome. In 2005, one study showed that 40% of major corporate chief executives outsourced or intended to outsource one or several units to a foreign country. While many jobs first migrated to Asia, they now also move to North Africa, central Europe or even the Caucasus. In 2005, Internet provider Lycos France, a subsidiary of Spanish group Telefonica, transferred a portion of its operations to Erevan, in Armenia.

This trend isn't limited to industry. In 2004, one in two firms was considering relocating a service activity. Today, one wage earner out of five in OECD countries works in an activity that could be outsourced.

Offshoring is a direct consequence of stepped-up globalisation from the 1990s onward. From the moment most obstacles to

international trade were lifted, communications became instantaneous, companies were able to establish themselves abroad easily
and production chains were globalised, companies couldn't wait to
seek out labour in least-cost countries.

The impact of offshoring on employment isn't straightforward.
Many companies only outsource part of their production to emerging countries. The jobs lost in this way are in labour-intensive, low-
skill areas such as assembly lines. The savings the company makes
in productivity, competitiveness, etc., allow it to make new investments. Its overall sales and turnover grow, allowing it to hire new
workers.

Job losses are not only due to globalisation

While offshoring is a highly visible symptom of the impact of globalisation on some job types, it is far from the only cause of job losses
in developed countries. In Europe, fewer than 5% of job losses in
industry and services can be explained by the decision to outsource
an activity to a lower-wage country. In France, offshoring caused
13 500 industrial job losses from 1995-2001 – a relatively low number compared with total job losses. A study over the period 2002-04
showed that 75% of European job losses were caused by internal
restructuring following technological or process improvements or
corporate strategic re-orientation, and 15% by bankruptcies.

In the United States, the share of job losses due to delocalisation is
also low – even if it has risen in recent years. In 2003, 13 000 job losses
– or less than 1% of total job losses – were due to offshoring. During the
first quarter of 2004 alone, the number of jobs eliminated due to offshoring had reached 2% of total job losses. As in Europe, most US job
losses resulted from productivity gains stemming from new technologies and from companies' strategic re-orientation.

Indeed, globalisation does have an impact on these factors. As
we've seen, the increased economic integration of countries promoted growth through productivity gains and the spread of new
technologies, allowing companies to realise considerable productivity gains. Job losses due to increased efficiencies, restructuring
and corporate bankruptcies can be viewed as *indirect* consequences
of globalisation. But these gains in efficacy and productivity also
create new jobs. In any event, the opening of borders to trade and
investment isn't the sole culprit.

Creation of new jobs in high-tech industries and services

The recent economic crisis caused a significant spike in unemployment in most OECD countries. While countries' growing interdependence made it easier for the shock to spread, the shock itself was caused by the malfunctioning financial sector and some macroeconomic imbalances (see Chapter 8). In the decade preceding the crisis, the total number of jobs in the OECD did not fall, quite the contrary – job losses in some sectors were compensated by millions of job creations.

New professions appeared, particularly in the services industry, which in Germany created 3 million jobs from 1995-2003. Business-to-business activities alone (accounting, human resources, call centres, web design, logistics, etc.), hotels and restaurants, health care and services to individuals created over 2.5 million positions. These new service professions often generate greater value-added than labour-intensive activities. The wealth thus created could be re-invested in new activities, which in turn create new jobs.

On average, the number of service-related jobs created in this way was greater than the number of lost industrial jobs in developed countries during the last decade. Between 1995 and 2005, the employment rate in OECD countries rose 1.1% annually. This progression is higher than the 1% annual population increase. This means that globalisation and competition from low-cost countries did not stop developed countries from creating more jobs. Better still, the resulting productivity gains led to new job creations in higher-value-added sectors. In 2007, just before the global economic crisis, the average unemployment rate of 5% in OECD countries was at its lowest since 1990.

In developing countries – and particularly emerging countries – globalisation led to job creation, either through new businesses being created or companies offshoring from developed countries. While it may be difficult to put a precise figure on this, it can be said that globalisation created more jobs overall than it destroyed.

But jobs are just one adjustment variable among others. Countries can't ignore globalisation's "losers". They must implement adjustment and training measures to meet the challenges of globalisation (see the conversation with Paul Swaim at the end of this chapter). And, what's more, the positive balance we refer to here only concerns employment *volume*. What about employment *quality*? This is where, more often than not, globalisation gets the blame.

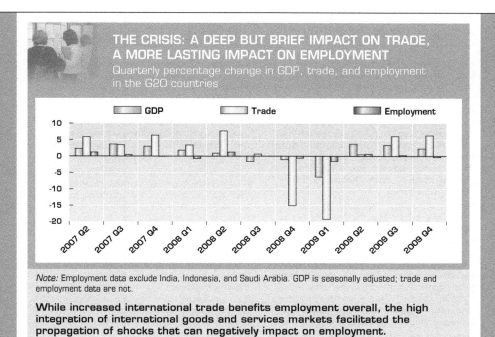

THE CRISIS: A DEEP BUT BRIEF IMPACT ON TRADE, A MORE LASTING IMPACT ON EMPLOYMENT

Quarterly percentage change in GDP, trade, and employment in the G20 countries

Note: Employment data exclude India, Indonesia, and Saudi Arabia. GDP is seasonally adjusted; trade and employment data are not.

While increased international trade benefits employment overall, the high integration of international goods and services markets facilitated the propagation of shocks that can negatively impact on employment.

Source: "Seizing the Benefits of Trade for Employment and Growth", joint report of the OECD, ILO, World Bank and WTO, available at *www.oecd.org/dataoecd/61/57/46353240.pdf*.
StatLink http://dx.doi.org/10.1787/888932780190

In real life

Albert Lebleu, 62 years old, former engineer at Metaleurop, Courcelles-lès-Lens, France

"The worst, for us, was that decisions were no longer made locally."

The road that leads to Courcelles-lès-Lens, in France's Nord-Pas-de-Calais, bears constant reminders of the region's historical milestones: its glory days, with its textile factories, its wealth, its coal mines. The volcano-like silhouette of the highest slag-heap in Europe (186 metres) brings to life the flat and monotonous terrain of this little corner of the northwest. In 1914, at the beginning of the First World War, the front line was 15 kilometres away. The area was

hit by cannonades. Men from over twelve countries and three continents killed each other in the environs during this time of globalised conflict. A military cemetry at the entrance to the town keeps alive the memory of the events.

Today, low houses emphasise the peaceful nature of this village of a few thousand souls. In a room on the first floor of the small city hall, Albert Lebleu busies himself in the middle of a *bric-à-brac* of cases, stacked chairs and ageless computers.

At 62 years old, this trained chemical engineer with greying hair is still full of energy. The various associations he heads, including that for former Metaleurop workers,

In real life (cont.)

keep him almost as busy as ever, but this time on a volunteer basis. His plant closed suddenly in 2003. After 33 years of loyal service to the Metaleurop Nord foundry, Albert Lebleu agreed to take early retirement. During those years, he witnessed the impact of globalisation on his company. Since joining in 1970, he held various posts. In 1975, his contribution to an internal research programme resulted in the company adopting a then-unique process in the field of germanium production. The patent still bears his name, along with the names of two colleagues who fine-tuned the process with him.

Today, there is pride in his eyes as he recounts his factory's past. In the 1960s, the Metaleurop foundry was the first to adopt the pyrolysis process for treating metals such as lead and zinc. This process was later implemented elsewhere, in Australia, North America... The booming company then changed its positioning to produce rarer metals. Metaleurop Nord was the largest global exporter of germanium, a metal used to make night-vision goggles. The factory produced a component used in liquid crystal monitors. "As a production unit, we were very technology-oriented", remembers Lebleu.

But 35 years ago, other countries started occupying the same niche, sometimes with more recent installations and technologies – the first signs of globalisation. "Our competitiveness started to erode", he relates. "First, Japan entered the competition in the 1970s. Then, China arrived on our markets in the 1980s, followed by India in the 1990s. To maintain our competitive edge, we had to step up equipment automation. In 1986, my team went from 19 to 16 employees." In three decades, the workforce was halved, from 1 600 to 830 employees. The pace picked up, along with stress. "Before, workers didn't drag their feet to come to work", he notes. "They enjoyed chatting over coffee breaks. But the pace just kept speeding up. These relaxing moments became increasingly rare. At the same time, the average age in the company kept rising as no new people were taken on", he continues. "In the early 2000s, the average age was 50. We had to preserve our market share to keep the factory going." But globalisation became more present and decisions were being made further and further away. "The factories started changing hands according to the mood of the financial markets."

In the mid-1990s, a Swiss group bought into Metaleurop's capital. "The foundry no longer interested the previous shareholder, a German industrial group

that made a 180-degree turn to focus on... tourism. The Swiss group became a major shareholder, with one-third of the capital. Very quickly, it froze investments. We felt we were losing control over our destiny. Financial holdings, with their army of lawyers, became the plant's real bosses", he protests. "Faced with these entities – some of them protected in tax havens – we couldn't do much. The problem is that globalisation happens quickly and that laws, behaviours and codes can't keep up."

In the meantime, the rising number of cheaper foundries in emerging countries meant that Metaleurop could no longer break even, and accounts plunged into the red. The company built up losses. "Early in 2003, the parent company turned off the tap", recounts Lebleu, as Metaleurop's majority shareholder dropped its subsidiary with no resources and without giving the workers any notice. At the time, there was no transnational legislation to force the parent company to honour the commitments of a subsidiary if it was not a majority shareholder. "From one day to the next, we found ourselves without jobs and without unemployment benefits. Management simply decided to abandon the production unit, hiding behind the fact that the coffers were empty at the branch level."

Metaleurop Nord was then known as one of Europe's most polluted sites. Hazardous chemicals were stored in the open and not one euro was spent on cleaning up. "We lived through savage capitalism in all its horror", judges Lebleu today. "With globalisation, capital came and went across borders. They could run a factory into the ground and leave behind an ecological and social disaster." Finally, the French authorities financed a portion of the decontamination process. Five years later, new activities have sprung up. Of the 830 employees of Metaleurop Nord, only 60 or so are still unemployed. "The social damages have been mitigated", concedes Lebleu.

Four years later, the retired engineer has found new occupations, but he now wonders about the future of his 35-year-old daughter, also an engineer. "In the early 1970s, fewer than 10% of people in my age range had earned the baccalaureate (the secondary education diploma). Today, nearly everyone has one. Becoming an engineer in no way guarantees you a good career – you have to prove yourself constantly. On top of that, our purchasing power is not keeping pace. More and more people work for the minimum wage. And globalisation doesn't help this at all", he concludes.

Globalisation seems to increase disparities in job quality

"In OECD countries, globalisation is found to have disproportionate impacts on certain types of workers, particularly low-skilled workers who may also be concentrated in certain regions."

OECD, *Staying Competitive in the Global Economy – Compendium of Studies on Global Value Chains*, 2008

Some fear that globalisation will lower employment standards – the "race to the bottom" – as workers in industrialised countries see their wages and work conditions align with those in low-wage countries. Is this fear founded?

Lower salaries in low value-added sectors

Wage levels in OECD countries present a mixed picture. Faced with international competition, some real wage concessions are taking place. Here again, offshoring has painful consequences. In 2008, the United Auto Workers (UAW) union of US automotive workers agreed to halve the wages of young workers to preserve employment at a Ford plant threatened with a transfer to Mexico. On the other side of the Rio Grande, Mexican workers' representatives made even greater concessions, with newly hired workers sometimes agreeing to start at USD 1.50 per hour. At that rate, a Mexican worker is competitive, even compared with a Chinese worker.

"One of the arguments for adopting the North America Free Trade Agreement (NAFTA) was that Mexican wages would climb gradually until they were the same as in the United States. Instead of there being upward pressure on Mexican wages, US wages were subjected to downward pressure."

Ben Davis, director of the Mexico City solidarity bureau of US union AFL-CI

The simple *threat* of offshoring is sometimes enough to lower employment quality in developed countries, because it reduces corporate union activism. As companies internationalised and outsourced a number of functions, the links between the top and the bottom of the pyramid grew looser – which caused wages to rise more slowly (see Albert Leleu's account above). Between 2001 and 2006, the real weekly wages of average US workers – those in the middle of the wage distribution range – decreased by 4%, despite a 15% productivity gain. In Germany and Japan, real wages stagnated. The overall result is that since the 1980s, the share of income from labour in OECD countries has declined. In contrast, in 2006 the share of company profits exceeded 15% of the GDP of the seven most industrialised countries, compared with 13% in the early 1980s.

Here too, of course, situations differ from one industry to another. The workers whose wages and working conditions are under pressure toil in industries competing with low-cost countries. Standardised and repetitive industrial and service jobs are under constant threat of relocation. Computing, chemicals or finance are not subjected to the same international pressure as more traditional sectors such as textiles, cars or electronics. On the contrary, wages in these sectors grew at the same time as globalisation intensified.

The impact of globalisation on wages in OECD countries is therefore mixed: while job quality has worsened in the now less-competitive sectors, many high-quality jobs have been created in sectors where these countries have a major comparative advantage in international markets. On the demand side, the development of emerging countries has offered new outlets for OECD area companies. With regard to the offer, international competition has made products and services more competitive and has resulted in the hiring of a better-trained and more productive workforce. Today, companies need an ever widening range of specialised skills. In 2006, jobs that demanded a high capacity for judgment represented over 40% of open corporate jobs in the United States and nearly 70% of overall jobs created since 1998. These kinds of job are more valued and generally better paid.

The result is the appearance of a two-speed labour market in OECD countries. On the one hand, the wages of unskilled workers have shrunk. On the other, the wages of educated and experienced workers in prime niches have soared. Wage inequalities have increased over the past decades. In 2006, the richest Americans earned the equivalent of 16% of all the income generated in the United States in a year, compared with only 8% in 1980. The income gap between the richest 10% of citizens and the poorest 10% has widened in developed countries, with some rare exceptions: in Ireland and Spain, that gap actually shrank between 1994 and 2005, their economic catching-up period.

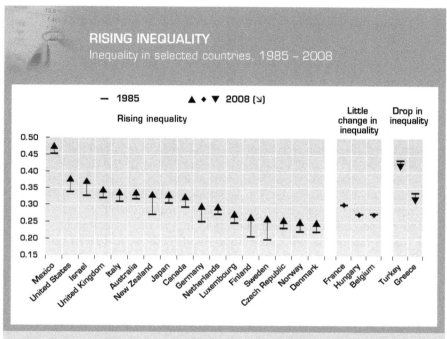

RISING INEQUALITY

Inequality in selected countries, 1985 – 2008

Note: For the Czech Republic and Hungary, the period under study started in the early 1990s, not in 1985.

NB: Temporary data from the *OECD Database on the Distribution of Income and Poverty.*

In most OECD countries, inequality grew between the mid-1980s (the average Gini coefficient was then 0.28) and the late 2000s (with an average 0.31 Gini coefficient). For a definition of the Gini coefficient, see the graph on the evolution of inequality in China and India in Chapter 5.

Source: OECD (2011), *Divided We Stand: Why Inequality Keeps Rising.*
StatLink http://dx.doi.org/10.1787/888932780209

But is this growing inequality only due to globalisation? According to the in-depth OECD study *Divided We Stand: Why Inequality Keeps Rising,* the relationship between inequality and globalisation and their effect on overall employment isn't that obvious. The study shows that the main factors behind wage disparities over the past decades at the global level have been institutional and political changes (especially labour market rules) and technological advances.

Some job insecurity

Wages aside, many workers and union representatives point to the increasing lack of job security. Here too, OECD firms' ability to offshore to low-wage countries with less rigid social legislation weakens unions' bargaining power and exerts downward pressure on employment quality.

OECD area companies increasingly resort to part-time work and fixed-term contracts. According to the European Trade Union Confederation (ETUC), of the 4 million jobs created in the European Union in 2006, the share of part-time jobs has grown. In 2008, 40 million EU workers held a part-time position, compared with 32 million ten years ago. Some 14.5% of European workers have a fixed-term contract, compared with 11.5% in 1997. According to ETUC, young people all over Europe – and up to 50% of 16-25 year olds – are subjected to this type of contract. In Sweden, 68% of young people work under a fixed-term contract.

The overall picture therefore reveals a degree of insecurity in unskilled jobs in OECD countries, partly linked to increased competition from low-wage countries – where laws and practices often give less protection to employees.

Improvement in job quality in emerging countries

One of the dark sides of globalisation is sweatshops – workshops run by the sub-contractors of major brands in which employees wear themselves down working long hours for subsistence wages. Likewise, child labour and modern slavery are realities in many countries. Some unscrupulous entrepreneurs settle in countries with such dire poverty that workers are willing to make considerable sacrifices. Sometimes, the global race for the lowest wages and least restrictive social legislation leads to situations where worker relations resemble the law of the jungle. Countries do not always have the administrative and legal infrastructure necessary to enforce the most basic employment laws.

Yet globalisation can also lead to improved employment conditions in developing and particularly emerging countries. Many MNEs that have settled there to manufacture and sell products and services have imported their original quality standards and good practices. Local companies that have entered into partnerships with MNEs have noticed higher levels of productivity than competitors who do not have this experience. Overall, MNEs pay their employees higher wages than local companies. Likewise, their unionisation rate is slightly higher, except in the Middle East.

That said, these positive repercussions may mostly benefit skilled workers, as opposed to manual workers performing minor or routine tasks. Recent studies in Brazil and Indonesia show that when a foreign company purchased a local business, wages quickly rose 10% to 20% on average. But we do not have accurate enough data to find out how these gains are distributed.

The improvements brought about by MNEs are not always automatic or spontaneous. The moral pressure exerted by NGOs, unions and civil society can produce higher wages and improved working conditions in MNE subsidiaries or local sub-contractors. In recent years, major international groups have established in-house corporate social responsibility programmes (CSR) which, while it may be good that they exist, are not always optimally effective on the ground – as witness the example of Nike (see the box).

Corporate social responsibility (CSR): A mixed review for Nike, Inc.

Nowadays, the impact of CSR programmes on working conditions seems limited. The main difficulty lies in elevating employment standards in a very tense competitive environment. Nike, the US manufacturer of sports equipment, is a case in point. The brand only has 24 000 direct employees. Almost all of its production is subcontracted to some 800 manufacturers in 51 countries. In the early 1990s, Nike was the target of a very negative media campaign because it was discovered that its subcontractors used underage workers. In reaction, Nike established a very strict supplier control system. In 2004, the firm employed 80 CSR supervisors and inspectors responsible for ensuring that subcontractors were respecting Nike's code of conduct on the ground. Despite this army of controllers, 80% of Nike's external suppliers failed to implement and follow the code prescribed by the US management. Controllers' visits have until now had a very limited effect.

By way of conclusion...

In order to make an objective assessment of the impact of globalisation on employment, we have to look at the bigger picture, This suggests that, overall, globalisation creates more jobs than it destroys. But this should not be cause for celebration. For the thousands of workers who lose their job or purchasing power due to company offshoring or loss of competitiveness, it is of no consolation whatsoever to know that there are plenty of vacancies and that wages are rising in other sectors or countries.

Governments cannot ignore globalisation's "losers" – those who work in sectors weakened by international competition. The 2008 economic crisis caused unemployment rates in the OECD area to soar. By the first quarter of 2010, employment had receded 2.1% over a period of two years and the unemployment rate had risen by slightly over 50% to 8.7% – or 17 million additional jobless.

The crisis led governments to take unprecedented steps to tackle unemployment and help workers weather the storm, compared to recent recessions. Three major types of measure were implemented which, while not specifically aimed at job losses linked to decreased international trade, did cover them.

First, governments (including Germany and several central European countries such as Hungary) sought to prevent job losses through part-time work programmes. These aimed to reduce working hours for the entire workforce, so long as economic difficulties lasted, in order to maintain jobs at the company. Since this meant lower wages, governments committed to make up some of the shortfall. As the goal of these public financing mechanisms is to preserve jobs that are viable over the long term, they must be time-limited (say, to one year), otherwise governments risk permanently financing jobs that are no longer competitive. The Netherlands went one step further: companies that laid off workers within six months of receiving the last subsidies had to refund the authorities half of the monies received.

Secondly, governments (including in Japan) aimed to support the unemployed proactively, by extending the available subsidies to include temporary workers who had lost their jobs. While often done on an *ad hoc* basis, this measure was still very useful to the most economically fragile jobless persons.

Finally, governments proactively increased their support for pro-grammes to help people return to work. Public budgets were consider-ably expanded, for example to hire more staff in public employment services. During periods of economic growth, governments should preferably focus on people's adaptability in terms of employment. In times of crisis, though, this isn't enough. They need to increase the number of training programmes and funding for work experience, etc.

Most of these measures have been temporary, because they were designed to respond to an exceptional situation. A number of govern-ments progressively adjusted or terminated them in order to maintain flexibility in the employment market and guarantee competitiveness.

Long-term measures capable of maintaining employment levels and reducing inequalities while preserving competitiveness are those included in redistributive social and fiscal policies, as well as – crucially – in dialogue among social partners (see the conversa-tion below with Paul Swaim). More importantly, governments must insist on life-long educational and training policies if they are to offer a better response to the negative effects of globalisation. This must be a priority, so that globalisation can promote employment – for both companies and workers.

A conversation

Paul Swaim, OECD Directorate for Employment, Labour and Social Affairs

"To remedy the negative effects of globalisation on employment in some sectors, we must help workers adapt their qualifications or expectations to the most promising employment sectors."

The financial then economic crisis, which originated in the United States, had a severe and unprecedented impact on most developed economies, which suffered record unemployment. Doesn't the crisis prove that globalisation destroys jobs?

The link between job losses and globalisation isn't as obvious as it seems. Of course, the crisis caused heavy job losses in most economies, particularly in some sectors like construction and industry. But job losses

in construction were less linked to international trade, while industry was more affected than expected. This is probably due to the drop in international trade, which was also steeper than expected.

That said, while international trade fell off dramatically in Germany, for example, unemployment rose relatively moderately. This was partly because employers adopted a long-term view and preferred to keep their workforce in order to be more competitive when recovery came.

Globalisation undeniably accelerated the spread of the crisis, first to the financial sector, then to companies, then to employment – with unexpected speed and gravity due to highly integrated production and trade networks in different countries.

A conversation *(cont.)*

We've seen recently that recovery in China and other emerging countries has played a major role in the strong recovery of Australia, Germany and Korea, thanks to their dynamic exports. But while globalisation can help spread the mishaps, it also spreads the benefits of periods of economic prosperity. In terms of the volume of employment, it seems to me that globalisation is more of a catalyst than an underlying cause.

But doesn't globalisation itself impact on the employment rate in certain sectors?

Globalisation goes hand in hand with decreased competitiveness of some industrial sectors like textiles or mass electronics in developed countries and hence, with job losses in these sectors. But it's hard to evaluate the impact of globalisation on job volume worldwide. Openness to the global market doesn't automatically lead to job losses. In the years that preceded the crisis, the more open countries – like Scandinavia or Switzerland, where wages are very high – did not experience a weaker employment market.

If we look at OECD countries since the early 1990s, employment levels rose before the crisis even as their economies were becoming increasingly integrated. After a peak in the early 2000s, the unemployment rate dropped. By 2007, at the height of the last economic cycle, the average unemployment rate in OECD countries had dropped to its lowest level since 1980. Trade liberalisation was also a means for a certain number of developing and emerging countries to create pressure to improve the jobs market and increase employment. But here again, this wasn't automatic. Many developing countries didn't benefit from globalisation because they didn't have the necessary preconditions, like an effective and impartial legal system.

Even if the relationship isn't automatic, it does seem that, overall, trade promotes employment gains and better living standards. It allows countries to develop specialties – hence, jobs – where they are the most competitive. In OECD countries, the term "creative destruction" is quite appropriate. Certainly, if governments establish adequate national policies to support growth and employment, globalisation should not deter from a consistently high employment level.

What about employment quality? Doesn't globalisation foster a race to the bottom?

Some pre-crisis concerns seem justified. Two wage indicators are quite worrying. First, the global share of wages and workers' compensation has been dropping in relation to GDP since the late 1980s. Globalisation is no stranger to this. Experts agree that increased trade with low-wage countries such as China or Central European nations, leads to a compression of wages in industrialised countries. As workers in low-wage countries today have the same competencies as unskilled workers in OECD countries, the unskilled workers' wages tend to drop.

Likewise, globalisation lowers the wage bargaining power of unions – in case of disagreement, employers can always threaten offshoring. But globalisation also increases many workers' purchasing power by lowering the prices of a range of consumer goods used in everyday life. Also, not all workers in developed countries lose out in terms of wages. Highly skilled workers in the high-tech sectors have had wage increases.

So employment quality evolves differently depending on the skill level?

This brings us to our second concern: the gap is widening between the top and the bottom of the wage pyramid. This phenomenon can be observed in two-thirds of OECD countries. The gap has been widening for quite a while already in the United States and United Kingdom. In Continental Europe, inequalities were less pronounced – but the wage gap has deepened in the past 20 years or so. Several studies show that the fragmentation of union power plays a major role in this respect.

A conversation *(cont.)*

The fact that the wage inequalities were less pronounced in Europe than in the United States was due mainly to unions having more centralised influence on wage determination. Scandinavian countries used to have a particularly advanced social consultation system. Now they are moving away from this model, decentralising further and giving more margin to sector discussions at lower levels. It's hard to predict for now how far this process will take them. But with rising international competition, solidarity among different social segments will probably not be as much a given as it was in the 1960s.

Of course, we can't align all wages, as it would have a negative impact on productivity and competitiveness. But to maintain an acceptable level of inequality, some mechanisms are less harmful to competitiveness – for example income transfers by public authorities, redistributive tax systems, support for education and training...

So it's been proven that globalisation increases wage inequalities?

Rising inequalities do not stem just from globalisation. In the United States, the consensus 10 years ago was that rising inequality was caused by the reduced power of unions and by globalisation (two related factors), as well as by technological evolution. It's quite clear that the changing nature of technology has become a major differentiating factor. Twenty years ago, knowing how to use a computer efficiently was not a decisive asset, whereas it most definitely is today. It's hard to determine which – globalisation or technology – has had more impact on employment. Nevertheless, we believe that technological development still has more influence on rising inequality than global economic integration.

Why is employment flexibility so vital?

With globalisation, some employment flexibility is vital to corporate competitiveness, hence growth, which in turn promotes employment. In countries such as France where layoffs are a complicated matter and existing jobs are highly protected, it's a lot harder to make a place for oneself on the job market. Which is why young people are increasingly turning to interim or temp work and internships until interesting jobs become available.

The recent economic crisis showed that this situation forces young workers to bear the lion's share of the flexibility burden. For example, during the last year of the crisis (from Q4 2008 to Q4 2009), the employment rate dropped 8.4% for workers aged under 25, compared with a 2.2% drop for workers aged 25 to 54 and a 1.7% hike for workers aged 55 and over. The result is very high unemployment among youth in some countries such as Spain, where one working-age youth out of two is unemployed. There is, however, an encouraging sign: some countries where this duality is pronounced are trying to introduce reforms to even out the employment protection offered to some categories of worker.

Is globalisation incompatible with job security?

That seems to be going too far. Some degree of flexibility is vital, but this doesn't mean that there should be no supportive measures in place – quite the contrary. Some countries have placed textile workers in training programmes. Others have set up training systems for older workers. Their success isn't always a given, as it's not easy to undergo training and master computer tools when school is a distant – and often not very positive – memory. It's all the more difficult as there is no guarantee that an employer will not choose to hire a 23-year-old with equal qualifications. Our research shows that the most effective solution is often to help unemployed workers find a position close to the one they held in their original sector. Of course, from a macroeconomic viewpoint it is better to help people move from declining sectors to developing sectors. But this doesn't necessary hold true at the microeconomic level.

A conversation *(cont.)*

Effective support measures can also include wage levels. Some countries test wage insurance systems, knowing that the job a person will find after a restructuring will often earn less than the previous one. The United States, France, Germany are testing such systems. In the United States, the company must prove that the restructuring was due to international competition. But here again, we don't have enough hindsight yet to evaluate the impact of these measures.

The measures that seemed most essential to countering the negative effects of globalisation on employment involve helping workers adapt their qualifications or expectations to the most promising employment sectors. Whatever the case may be, the best solution isn't to close oneself to international trade, but rather to offer the best possible educational level to young generations and life-long training to workers – in short, to allow people to climb the social ladder rather than tumble down to the lower wages.

Is a good education sufficient to find a job today?

University graduates do not feel as privileged as they used to. They are feeling more insecure. Previously, 10% of the population went to university. Now, it's 50% – even 80% in some countries. Yet senior management and executive positions are not more plentiful, and a huge gap has arisen in some countries between supply and demand for them. Over-qualification – where people are considered too skilled to fit a position – is also a cause of unemployment.

International competition is increasing even in sectors that require a high level of qualifications. An Indian physician can now analyse scans taken in Austria. This was unimaginable only 10 years ago, when Western specialists could not even imagine having to compete one day with radiologists in Mumbai! More and more, people want life-long training so that they can adapt to major technological, economic and social evolutions. Clearly, governments must play a role in this respect.

That said, even though the race for university degrees and international competition has risen in the OECD area, there is still a higher likelihood of finding employment if people have a higher-education degree than if they are low-skilled. Moreover, university graduates' difficulties in finding work quickly are more often related to inadequate employment policies than to globalisation.

Find out more

FROM OECD...

On the Internet

The OECD website's "Trade and Jobs" page summarises the organisation's analyses on globalisation's impact on employment and provides varied, clear and useful sources: *www.oecd.org/trade/tradeandjobs.htm.*

OECD work on employment is available at: *www.oecd.org/employment.*

International Collaborative Initiative on Trade and Employment (ICITE): A joint initiative of 10 international organisations including the OECD, the World Bank and the World Trade Organization (WTO), the ICITE aims to provide a better understanding of how trade interacts with employment; promote dialogue on these issues; and to develop policy-relevant conclusions: *www.oecd.org/trade/ICITE* (in English only).

Publications

OECD Employment Outlook 2011: An annual report of the OECD on employment in OECD countries and beyond. The 2011 edition focuses on the impact of the global economic crisis. While most economies are experiencing a surge in production, employment will take longer to recover. Chapter 1 evaluates how the safety net functioned in OECD countries in the throes of the "Great Recession". Chapter 2 analyses the effect of social protection systems on the employment market in emerging economies.

Divided We Stand: Why Inequality Keeps Rising (2011): This OECD book examines to what extent economic globalisation, technological advances based on competencies and institutional and regulatory reforms have had an impact on wage distribution.

Globalisation, Employment and Wages (2007): This OECD *Policy Brief* reviews among others the consequences of increased international competition on employment levels and studies the evolution of real wages in OECD countries in recent years.

... AND OTHER SOURCES

Prospects for Foreign Direct Investment and the Strategies of Transnational Corporations (2005-08): This report of the United Nations Conference on Trade and Development provides insight to understand the strategies of companies undergoing offshoring and their obvious effects on employment in the country they are leaving.

7

Globalisation helped accentuate the major environmental damages we're experiencing today, even though it's only indirectly responsible. Some national, regional and international policies have attenuated the negative effects of globalisation on the environment. Some solutions can also be found in the mechanisms of globalisation itself. But while vital, political regulations and incentives are still lacking compared to the breadth and urgency of the challenges ahead.

What is
the impact of
globalisation on
the environment?

By way of introduction...

At the Avoriaz ski station on the border between France and Switzerland, planted between a cliff and a huge rocky outcrop at an altitude of 1 800 metres, winters vary from year to year. Shopkeepers and the tourism office yearn for their increasingly rare white gold. In the 1970s, annual cumulated snowfall was as high as 13 metres. Today, it never goes above 8 metres. So Avoriaz is trying to diversify its activities, investing more in summer tourism and ecology. Part of this strategy involves building a state-of-the-art water sports complex.

The years 1994, 2000, 2002 and 2003 saw the hottest temperatures in 500 years. The 2006 season was even worse. Ski lift orders in French ski stations dropped 22% compared with the previous year. No one is panicking – yet. "The most plausible hypothesis is that temperatures will rise two to three degrees in the years to come", states Guy Vaxelaire, secretary of the national association of French ski station mayors. "From a statistical standpoint, this would boost the ratio of bad to good seasons from 1 in 10 to 2 in 10, which is still manageable." Perhaps so, but a general 1° temperature rise would shut down over 160 ski areas out of the existing 666 in the Alps. According to the OECD, German ski stations are even more at risk.

There's international consensus on the existence of global warming and its increase since the 1980s. The average atmospheric temperature is rising, particularly in the Northern hemisphere. While the scientific community is divided as to exactly how much humans are to blame for global warming, the vast majority nevertheless agree that it's very real. Most scientists – especially those working in the Intergovernmental Panel on Climate Change (IPCC) – believe that increases in emissions of carbon dioxide (CO_2) from human activity are the primary cause of global warming.

Yet global warming isn't the only environmental problem. Industry, mass consumption and the increased energy needs of a growing global population are partly responsible for pollution, resource depletion and species extinction. Globalisation has occurred alongside and sometimes nurtured these developments.

This chapter summarises the main impacts of globalisation on the environment. Awareness has grown in recent years, but is still not enough. It should be possible not only to reconcile globalisation and conservation of the environment, but also to act so that globalisation becomes a vector of green growth.

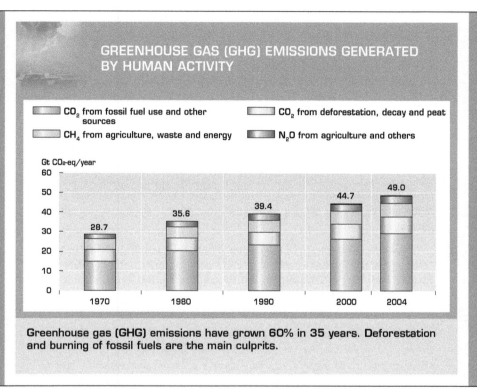

GREENHOUSE GAS (GHG) EMISSIONS GENERATED BY HUMAN ACTIVITY

▦ CO₂ from fossil fuel use and other sources

▦ CH₄ from agriculture, waste and energy

▦ CO₂ from deforestation, decay and peat

▦ N₂O from agriculture and others

Gt CO₂-eq/year

1970: 28.7
1980: 35.6
1990: 39.4
2000: 44.7
2004: 49.0

Greenhouse gas (GHG) emissions have grown 60% in 35 years. Deforestation and burning of fossil fuels are the main culprits.

Source: IPCC, *Climate Change 2007: Synthesis Report*, p. 36. Contribution of Working Groups I, II and III to the Fourth Assessment Report of the Intergovernmental Panel on Climate Change, Figure RiD.3(a), IPCC, Geneva, Switzerland.

Globalisation is partly responsible for environmental damage

Globalisation, which is partly synonymous with rising international trade, has fostered the rapid production, trade and consumption of material goods in unprecedented quantities. This has weighted the ecological footprint of human activities around the world. While it's still difficult to assess the impact of globalisation on the environment, it's quite obvious in some areas.

By increasing GHG emissions

Climate change is one of the main environmental problems, perhaps all the more worrying because it is impossible to predict exactly how it's going to develop and what the consequences will be. Its causes, however, are known. Climate change stems mostly from the greenhouse effect – meaning the excessive retention of solar energy in the atmosphere due to an accumulation of certain gases, particularly CO_2.

The main sources of CO_2 emissions are industrial production, transportation and, more indirectly, deforestation. These three human activities exist independently of globalisation, but their considerable development during the 20th century, and in particular in recent decades, is partly linked to accelerated globalisation.

Globalisation promotes CO_2 emissions from transport. As critical drivers of globalisation, transport systems have multiplied alongside international trade. Emissions from road transport (mainly cars and lorries) are of course very high, but more so within national borders. But the opening of some regional areas (such as the suppression of border controls among European Union countries) has given a strong boost to road freight transport. Despite some encouraging recent alternatives such as piggybacking (transporting lorries by train for part of the journey), transnational road transport is an important source of CO_2 emissions.

But the major mode of transport that has characterised globalisation in the past decades is the aeroplane. Between 1990 and 2004, GHG emissions from aviation increased 86%. Aviation is today responsible for 4-9% of total GHG emissions released into the atmosphere. Meanwhile, sea transport swallows 2-4% of all the fossil fuels consumed by the planet every year. Some 70% of international transport of goods towards the EU and 95% of trade towards the United States is by sea. Improved energy technologies aren't enough to absorb the environmental impact of the 3% annual increase in shipping.

That said, much of the environmental harm from transport is due to the increase in *domestic* traffic. In the case of aviation, between 2005 and 2007 Indian airline companies ordered a whopping 500 new aeroplanes from aircraft constructors Airbus and Boeing to cover new domestic travel needs. In other words, increased traffic on the highways of international trade, driven by the globalisation dynamic, isn't solely responsible for increases in transport-related CO_2 emissions.

Globalisation indirectly promotes CO_2 emissions linked to industrial activity and consumption. While the Industrial Revolution was a vector of globalisation (see Chapter 2), the growth in cross-border trade and investment in turn fostered industrial activity. This is often a major source of GHG emissions, as in the case of electricity generation, which still largely involves burning coal, oil and derivates. The intensification of globalisation, then, accentuated the greenhouse effect and global warming.

For decades, developed countries – the pioneers of global industrialisation – were the world's biggest polluters, responsible for the lion's share of GHG emissions. Today, the United States is responsible for around 20% of global GHG emissions.

But the very rapid development of emerging countries over the past several years has also led them to become major emitters of GHG. As we've seen, these countries developed largely thanks to globalisation, which fostered the industrialisation of the Asian giants – often at the expense of the environment. To quench its thirst for energy, China opens one new coal-fired power plant every week. Yet while coal is the cheapest and most abundant fossil fuel, it's also the most polluting... Add to that China's mushrooming transport fleet and galloping urbanisation and it became the world's largest emitter of CO_2, ahead of the United States, in 2007. Agreed, China has also embarked on drastic renewable energy programmes in recent years. But each day, emerging countries buy a little more into the logic of mass consumption linked to globalisation. This means that they will largely be responsible for rising GHG emissions in the years to come (see the conversation with Brendan Gillespie at the end of the chapter).

Globalisation encourages deforestation. Deforestation is an indirect but very significant cause of the greenhouse effect. Clearing and logging reduce the volume of CO_2 that plants convert into oxygen. This translates into an equivalent increase in the volume of CO_2 in the atmosphere and thus adds to the greenhouse effect. And burning the cleared wood releases vast quantities of CO_2. In total, estimated emissions from deforestation represent some 20% of the increased concentration of GHG in the atmosphere. Between 1990 and 2005, the world lost 3% of its forests. Some 200 km^2 of forest land – twice the size of Paris – disappears each day.

Globalisation is often an ally of the chainsaw. Deforestation is mainly due to the conversion of forests into agricultural land, especially in developing countries. Take Brazil: for a little over a decade, much of its agriculture was export-oriented. Between 1996 and 2003, Brazilian soy exports to China rocketed from 15 000 to 6 million tonnes. This dynamism involved deforestation and converting part of the rainforest into farmland.

Like much of the damage caused to the environment, the impact of deforestation isn't only felt by nature itself, but also by people, in particular the most vulnerable. The poorest regions are the most affected by global warming. In the medium term, the UN doesn't rule out a poverty boom stemming from desertification and increasingly scarce water. By 2060, drought could render 90 million hectares in sub-Saharan Africa sterile. Some 1.8 billion people could lack water in the next 70 years. Central Asia, northern China and the Andes are particularly at risk.

Furthermore, global warming may well be one of the causes of the increase in the number of natural disasters such as hurricanes, storms and floods in recent years. Approximately 262 million people worldwide were victims of natural disasters between 2000 and 2004.

Add to this the fact that 20% to 30% of all living species could disappear if the mean global temperature were to rise by 3 °C and it becomes clear that nature didn't need this: apart from global warming, 20th-century human activity already left an indelible mark on the world's ecosystems.

By impoverishing biodiversity

A large number of species have become extinct in recent decades. Again, the link between the extinction of some species and globalisation is indirect. Human activities (particularly industry, because of its pollution of ecosystems), urban sprawl, farms and mining – which displace certain species – are not in and of themselves the result of globalisation. But globalisation implies the multiplication of distribution channels, creating new needs and new demand for products that are used around the world. It accentuates industrialisation and the quest for and exploitation of new lands, subsoil and resources, thus weakening many ecosystems.

The example of fishing is particularly telling. Overfishing has emptied the oceans of some fish species. Stocks of Atlantic cod – formerly one of the most abundant species in Canadian waters – collapsed in the 1970s, decimated by overfishing and rising global demand. Mediterranean bluefin tuna has met with the same fate. Considered a delicacy in Japan, it's threatened with extinction from overfishing.

According to the International Union for Conservation of Nature (IUCN), 22% of the world's mammals are threatened with extinction today, as well as 24% of the world's snake species, 31% of the world's amphibians and 35% of the world's birds.

Flora are also at risk. Open international markets and lower communications prices have made some exotic raw materials and farm products affordable to consumers of developed countries. Rising demand slowly accentuated pressure on some plants. Take the island of Borneo. Popular taste for exotic wood furniture and other utensils has pushed some kinds of wood, like teak, into the threatened species category. Furthermore, the growing reliance of agribusiness on palm oil and the needs of the paper industry are at the root of the gigantic deforestation of Borneo's rainforest. Add galloping urbanisation and, at this pace, one-quarter of Borneo's flora and fauna will be wiped from the surface of Earth in a few years' time. The forest has retreated more quickly in the past 15 years in the South Pacific and South Asia than anywhere else on Earth. Forests in Latin America and sub-Saharan Africa are also being ravaged.

Like most major environmental problems, this predictable cataclysm of biodiversity has an economic cost. A drop in the pollination of flora (including crops) could cause a fall in yields. Countries will need to invest more in water purification, etc. According to some estimates, the total damages to the ecosystem would result in an annual loss of USD 68 billion to the world economy.

The positive spiral of development, which itself is partly linked to globalisation, is faced with a huge challenge. At this rate, the

World Wildlife Fund for Nature (WWF) predicts that by 2030, if nothing changes, humanity will exhaust annually twice the resources produced by the planet every year.

Uneven political efforts

For several decades, we've witnessed some degree of environmental awareness among political decision makers. While part of the damage to the environment stems directly or indirectly from globalisation, solutions can also be found in heightened international political co-operation. But all levels of decision making have to be mobilised.

As is the case for development and employment, **it's partly up to _national_ political decision makers to take pro-environmental measures to prevent or repair the environmental damage arising, in part, from globalisation**.

That there has been an increase in awareness of the need to conserve biodiversity can be seen in the growing number of protected natural areas worldwide since the last century. Since the end of the Second World War, the number of reserves and protected natural areas has multiplied almost twentyfold. In 2006, some 20 million km^2 of land and water were protected – more than twice the size of China. But vast swathes of the globe are still vulnerable and unprotected. Conserving the rain forest remains a challenge in the Amazon (see the conversation with Brendan Gillespie at the end of the chapter). Brasilia has promised to reduce by 70% the impact of clearing the Amazonian rainforest by 2018.

There are many national measures – particularly but not only in developed countries – to combat global warming and limit CO_2 emissions. They include compulsory catalytic converters on automobiles, particle filters for industry, subsidies to insulate buildings and avoid energy loss, etc. It's impossible to draw up an exhaustive list of all the environmental obligations or incentives aimed at companies and individuals in OECD countries. But there can be no doubt that in the past 30 years or so, domestic measures and campaigns have borne some fruits, at least with regard to raising awareness. In the OECD area, the average citizen has never been so preoccupied as today with preserving the habitat.

But one of the features of environmental damage is that it doesn't stop at borders. This means that it's sometimes necessary to resort to *bilateral* (between two countries) or *regional* (among countries of a same geographic area) agreements. This has happened in the past, with some success. For several decades, industrial emissions from US factories created chemical particle clouds that provoked acid rainfalls as they moved across Canadian regions bordering the United States. In 1991, an air quality agreement between the two countries imposed strict controls on industrial emissions. Since then, acid rainfalls have become much more rare. In addition, some bilateral trade agreements now include environmental clauses, such as withdrawing subsidies for activities that have negative impacts on the environment.

Some rules adopted at the *regional* level are the concrete expression of a desire to protect the environment. One such example is the European Union REACH programme, which aims to limit the proliferation of dangerous or potentially dangerous chemical substances. This programme led to a European directive whose implementation is strictly controlled – sometimes to the chagrin of European industrialists, who bemoan the loss of competitiveness resulting from these regulations compared with competitors from other regions who don't apply the same restrictions. This argument poses the fundamental question of the usefulness of environmental regulations if they're limited to a number of world regions. Some environmental challenges, such as global warming, are borderless and cannot be resolved by bilateral or regional agreements alone.

Some *globally* co-ordinated actions have positive results. Several countries have signed agreements restricting nitrogen dioxide (NO_2) emissions, the main culprits of acid rains – which are now considerably rarer throughout the world. The same goes for chlorofluorocarbons (CFC) emitted by refrigeration systems. CFC emissions, which are responsible for a worrying degradation of the ozone layer (which protects Earth's surface from dangerous solar radiations), have been drastically reduced by the Montreal protocol signed by many governments in 1987. In 2006, the World Meteorological Organization (WMO) noted that the ozone layer was reconstituting itself at the poles. When the international community gets going, it can achieve some environmental successes.

But **international co-operation on environmental matters is still insufficient.** Such is the case for global warming. And yet since the late 1980s, governments have begun to co-operate in an unprecedented manner on this crucial problem. First, the creation of the IPCC within the framework of the UN allowed global scientists to analyse the causes of warming, as we saw in the introduction to this chapter. Then, the 1992 Rio conference enabled over 150 governments to initiate a process whose first concrete advances were enshrined in the 1997 Kyoto Protocol. Through this treaty, each developed country committed to reducing its CO_2 emission levels for 2008-12 by 5% on average compared with its 1990 level.

Despite this unprecedented mobilisation of the international community and the proven efficacy of some measures, such as emission rights trading schemes, the Kyoto protocol is not enough. The United States, for example, did not sign it. In addition, the treaty did not bind developing countries, since it focused on the main emitters of CO_2. Yet as we've seen, emerging countries have also become important CO_2 emitters.

Many viewed the Copenhagen conference of December 2009, which was supposed to extend the dynamic of Kyoto, as a failure, mainly because the 180 governments involved did not reach a quantified agreement on GHG reductions. The 2010 Cancun conference and 2011 Durban conference partly remedied Copenhagen's failings: it set the goal of not exceeding a mean global warming of 2 °C compared with pre-industrial levels and created several tools to orchestrate countries' actions in this regard, according to development level. The Rio+20 agreement signed in June 2012 did not make any major progress.

Despite being disappointing, the international agreements on climate from Kyoto to Durban had the merit of making sure politicians were aware of the environmental stakes. The simple fact that the heads of state of the most polluting countries meet in the same room to address environmental questions is considerable progress in itself.

The result of the national and international measures taken over the past decades is that **for the past 30 years, developed countries have been polluting at a slower pace**. Since 1980, the ecological footprint of developed countries has been dissociated from growth in GDP (see graph). As for GHG reductions, these stemmed in part from the passage from an industrial economy to a service economy – by definition less polluting.

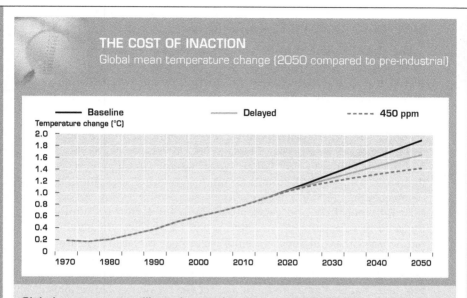

THE COST OF INACTION
Global mean temperature change (2050 compared to pre-industrial)

Global temperature will continue to increase until 2020. Then, everything will depend on the effectiveness and ambition of GHG emission-reduction plans. The baseline scenario reflects the possible development if nothing changes. The "450 ppm" scenario is the most ambitious of the three and presupposes the progressive establishment of a tax to limit long-term atmospheric concentrations of 450 parts per million (ppm) of CO_2 equivalent. This would result in emission reductions of about 40% in 2050 compared with 2000 levels.

Source: OECD (2008), *Environmental Outlook to 2030*, OECD Publishing, Paris.
StatLink http://dx.doi.org/10.1787/888932780228

Globalisation is a vector
for environmental solutions

As we've seen, globalisation is indirectly responsible for environmental damage. As with other areas, such as development, employment and finance, it makes both problems and benefits more apparent. Yet globalisation can also help lessen and prevent environmental damage. For example, international trade can help spread the most sophisticated environmental solutions far and wide, particularly with regard to global warming.

The globalisation of trade and research also applies to green technologies. Industry, global capital movements, and globalised research and innovation, can help promote sources of "green growth" and are particularly effective instruments to fight pollution and climate change on a global scale.

Public and private international investments in environmental technologies are ever higher. In late 2008, US venture capital funds had invested close to USD 2.8 billion in green technologies around the world – a record, despite difficult market conditions. Biofuels, renewable energy, wind energy and above all solar energy are on a roll. Between July and September 2008, total venture capital invested in solar energy amounted to USD 1.5 billion. In parallel, public investment in environmental technology research increased. The dynamism of "green" research and industry is promising: the quest for environmental solutions fosters new activities and new products, but also new production processes, which globalisation's trade and production network can help circulate quickly.

Globalisation can make environmental conservation compatible with development. International economic competition partly gets in the way of resolving environmental problems. Companies balk at spending money on environmental efforts, which means losing ground in this competition. Developing countries consider that developed countries are the main culprits and view the environmental efforts they are being asked to make as a means for the more advanced countries to maintain their economic head start. Yet environmental solutions must include international market mechanisms.

The CO_2 emission rights trading system set up under the Kyoto protocol is a perfect match for the globalisation dynamic. This system can be implemented among companies in various countries. It can include companies from developing countries and stimulate green investment in developing countries. In addition to the right to trade emissions permits, the Kyoto protocol includes an incentive system to increase developing countries' contribution to reducing GHG emissions while stimulating their economies: the Clean Development Mechanism (CDM) allows companies in developed countries to receive additional emission rights when they invest in less polluting industrial projects in developing countries. There have been some positive results, especially in China, but the process could be improved by simplifying some procedures and including more developing countries.

Independently of these mechanisms (which require some kind of preliminary institutional framework) corporate globalisation promotes clean technology transfers from developed to developing countries. MNEs, which for a long time didn't worry much about the environment, can also be precious allies in combating global warming. As they are knowledgeable about environmental standards and practices in developed countries, they are important vectors for transferring green technology and good-practice. Today, major European companies equip Chinese megalopolises with wastewater treatment plants and waste collection and recycling systems using cutting-edge technologies.

Despite their failings, the Copenhagen, Cancun and Rio agreements do stipulate that international aid for development, one of the facets of financial globalisation, shall focus more on economic programmes that promote environmental conservation. In addition, environmental awareness campaigns by NGOs are changing attitudes little by little, in the North as well as in the South.

On the whole, these developments have promoted some environmental awareness in emerging countries. During the Beijing Olympic Games, the Chinese authorities introduced a partial ban on car traffic in the city. Decision makers are increasingly concerned with the environment. The significant increase in pollution-related illnesses and ensuing public health costs are also incentives for political action.

By way of conclusion...

GHG emissions will continue to grow. The planet's mean temperature will rise, as will the loss of biodiversity. The extent of these increases will depend on the ambition and effectiveness of the measures to be adopted globally. Strong political will could slow down the phenomenon. Governments, companies and citizens must do more in many areas. They must consider all the stakes in order not to waste their energies, and insist on the least costly actions. Better yet, they should conceive, implement and promote actions that both protect the environment and create wealth and employment. This is the spirit of "green growth" advocated by the OECD and many international organisations.

Global warming is an urgent challenge to which global decision makers are not paying sufficient attention. Globalisation is compatible with a healthy and resource-rich environment that can sustainably satisfy the needs of future generations – provided it follows a sustainable path.

A conversation

Brendan Gillespie, Head, Environmental Performances and Information division, OECD Environment Directorate

What is the impact of globalisation on the environment?

There's no single answer to that question. As a growth-stimulating factor, globalisation impacts on the environment. At the same time, thanks to globalised information and knowledge, the public is considerably more aware of ecological issues and this has generated greater mobilisation. Theoretically, resources can be used more rationally because of increased trade and investment. But for the moment, it seems that globalisation's negative environmental effects are more apparent. For example, increased pollution linked to transport immediately comes to mind.

Is the growing share of transport in total global CO_2 emissions one of the causes of heightened global warming?

Transport's share in total CO_2 emissions has increased in recent years, but remains weak in absolute terms. There is much talk of "carbon kilometres" to assess international trade's ecological footprint. Some believe that in order to limit CO_2 emissions, Europeans should choose local wines over Chilean wines and stop buying Kenyan flowers. But these approaches are often short-sighted because they do not take the global picture into account. For example, cultivating flowers in Kenya consumes less total fossil energy than cultivating them in northern Europe, transport included.

Some believe that carbon sequestration technology could be perfected by 2020. At the same time, coal consumption could quadruple in China. Many are betting that improved technologies will provide solutions to global warming that we cannot even imagine yet. Can we afford to wait for these technologies?

True, technological innovation can play a major role in combating climate change. Policies that promote green technologies are multiplying. If the existing clean technologies were more widely available, we would already be seeing drastically reduced CO_2 emissions. A classic example: if all television sets and computers had a switch that automatically turned off the power supply, the energy savings would be huge.

Another example: incandescent light bulbs, which consume more energy and have a shorter lifespan than energy-saving bulbs, are now banned in Australia.

As for water resources, we are seeing huge waste in many developing countries, which use – often not very efficiently – 70% of their available water for agriculture. The problem stems in part from the very low cost of water to users. If these farmers used proven drip techniques more extensively, like in Australia and Israel, they would save millions of litres. Of course, this would require investments, but given the long-term real costs of current consumption modes, the return on investment would be significant.

A conversation *(cont.)*

Who should pay for these investments?

At the OECD, we have long insisted on the "polluter-payer" and "user-payer" principles. Environmental policies should make product costs reflect environmental costs. At the same time, consumers should pay for some environmental services, such as access to drinking water. Transporting water from a reservoir to a kitchen costs a lot of money.

It's true that the required investments can be so costly that they will only be amortised after 30 or 40 years, so it's probably preferable to consider water infrastructures as "public goods" and mobilise public funds to finance them. The same goes for health care. Pollution causes many respiratory illness in China. The World Bank estimated that if the country could improve the situation on this front it could gain 3-5% in GDP, thanks to savings in its health care system. Likewise, if we continue to raze the forests and sell off their resources at low cost, we won't have any forest reserves left very soon. We are mortgaging future gains. Sustainable management, on the other hand, will provide long-term revenues.

The difficulty stems from a lack of control over the criminal organisations that devastate nature reserves. International reports probably do not stress enough the illegal trade in plants and animals. The market is gigantic, and the damages huge. Africa, Indonesia and Russia, among others, suffer greatly from this kind of trafficking and lack the means to control it and stamp it out. A few years ago, some streets of Abidjan in the Ivory Coast were covered in toxic residue from a Dutch ship claiming to carry municipal waste. The risks that polluters run are low. Barring global policies and an international police force with appropriate means of enforcement, they will always win. There has been some progress, for example the collaboration between customs authorities and Interpol, but much remains to be done.

At the international level, investment financing is even more complicated. Historically, developed countries were the most responsible for GHG emissions. But in the future, developing countries will need to reduce their GHG emissions, with important implications for their development. Disagreements between developed and developing countries on responsibilities and cost sharing are major stumbling blocks in discussions about an international agreement on climate change.

Who has the power to turn today's planetary ecological degradation around?

First, the governments, which must take appropriate measures reflecting the environmental cost of the activities of public administrations, companies and citizens. But all the stakeholders must play a role: manufacturers must adopt production methods that are more respectful of the environment and consumers must change their habits, for example by purchasing "greener" products and services. Things are more complex than it seems. For example, encouraging companies or authorities to sell coffee branded "fair trade" may be good for the environment, but will not resolve all the environmental problems linked to coffee production. To have a truly positive impact, a palette of different measures will need to be implemented simultaneously.

How are developing countries raising awareness of environmental challenges?

GHG emissions occur in every country. OECD economies have been the main culprits, as well as the richest. In the future, GHG increases will come essentially from BRIC countries. But these will not become as rich as developed countries. We have a common – if deferred – responsibility. Environmental efforts must reflect these developments.

The Chinese authorities are today very aware of the need to act. Chinese industry consumes an abundance of raw materials. Their extreme dependence on external suppliers is a handicap – which is why Beijing has decided to invest in a more efficient production system, especially with regard to energy. Likewise, untreated waste water can be used for agriculture. Finally, the public is increasingly concerned about ecology.

A conversation *(cont.)*

Many Chinese media and households expressed deep displeasure when it appeared that some officials were closely linked to companies that had caused extreme pollution.

Despite this progress, some maintain that 80% of future increases in GHG emission will come from emerging countries...

There needs to be some arbitration between economic development and environmental challenges. Things are evolving and some countries are truly concerned. In 2008, the Brazilian minister of the environment quit because she was unable to enforce the Brasilia commitments. She believed that growth was being promoted at the expense of ecology. At the time, that gesture sent a strong message.

Isn't that actually a pessimistic signal?

Protecting the environment has a cost, but also generates often unknown benefits. As the Stern report clearly stated, prolonged inaction in environmental matters will end up costing us more than energetic action. We must identify the most effective instruments. Likewise, we must identify the potential winners and losers of environmental measures and mitigate their negative impacts on the groups suffering the most serious effects. Governments and companies increasingly recognise that respecting the environment doesn't just create costs, but that investing in it can provide a head start in future markets. The OECD Green Growth Strategy stresses this point.

Find out more

FROM OECD...

On the Internet

OECD work on green growth:
www.oecd.org/greengrowth.

OECD work on the environment:
www.oecd.org/environment.

Publications

Towards Green Growth (2011): This report presents the first conclusions of the OECD Green Growth Strategy centred on the synergies between economic and environmental policies. It explains how barriers to trade and investment can hinder the development and circulation of green technologies around the world. It also promotes the role of international financial flows (especially public development subsidies) in driving growth and development and enhancing the quality of public goods globally.

The Economics of Climate Change Mitigation: Policies and Options for Global Action Beyond 2012 (2010): This report explores available solutions for reducing GHG emissions at least cost and makes suggestions for developing a global carbon market.

Invention and Transfer of Environmental Technologies (2011): This report analyses the role of multilateral agreements, environmental policies and international markets in technological innovation and transfers. It notes that most technology transfers are performed through trade, FDI and patents.

Greening Household Behaviour: The Role of Public Policy (2011): This publication presents the main results and policy

implications of an OECD survey of more than 10 000 households in 10 countries. It offers new insight into what policy measures really work, looking at what factors affect people's behaviour towards the environment.

OECD Environmental Outlook to 2030 (2008): This OECD report analyses in depth the environmental challenges governments will face by 2030. It contains many examples and projection tables.

"Innovation, globalisation and the environment", *OECD Observer* No. 261, May 2007: In this article, Brendan Gillespie and Xavier Leflaive explain how the dissemination of new green technologies through globalisation networks could provide a partial solution to reducing GHG emissions in the medium term.

... AND OTHER SOURCES

Climate Change 2007, IPCC Fourth Assessment Report: This IPCC report on climate change is the leading reference on global warming.

Exploring trade and the Environment: An Empirical Examination of Trade Openness and National Environmental Performance (2011): This Yale University study evaluates the environmental impact of international trade and investment. It concludes that while this impact is positive with regard to health, it is rather negative for ecosystem vitality. It also highlights the crucial role of good governance in deriving benefits from international trade while reducing its environmental impact. See: *http://envirocenter.yale.edu/programs/en vironmental-performance-management/exploring-trade-and-the-environment.*

8

The 2007-08 financial crisis affected many countries simultaneously and led to a global economic crisis unseen since the Great Depression. It was triggered by a proliferation of financial products linked to risky mortgage loans. The crisis seriously called into question financial globalisation, which to a certain extent amplified risks linked to banking activities and financial markets and brought about financial imbalances among leading economic powers. The question of what rules should apply to global financial activity is crucial in channelling the risks inherent to globalisation.

The 2008 financial crisis – A crisis of globalisation?

By way of introduction...

"For the moment, we're sticking together, but who knows how long that will last?" Arnaud Lemoine, 35, an engineer at Renault, summarises the state of mind of many Renault employees – both manual workers and executives – in April 2009. During a management meeting, Arnaud learns that in order to maintain jobs during the economic turmoil arising from the financial crisis, employees earning in excess of a given salary are encouraged to reduce their working hours – which also implies reduced wages. "It's not catastrophic. I still have work... But it still feels strange."

That same month before the "Arab spring", Ali El Awary, 43, the owner of a *narghile* and oriental crafts shop on El-Mouiz street in old historic Cairo, rails against his bank. "I wanted to diversify by opening a restaurant near Zamalek. When I mentioned the project to my banker about six months ago, he was enthusiastic. But since the crisis, banks no longer want to extend credit." To top it all off, with a drop in tourism because of the crisis, his turnover dropped 35% in 2009. "That doesn't help me put over the case for my project to the bankers. They speculated, they failed, and now they're making us pay the price for their fall."

Reality has been even worse for others. Ratry Sovath, 37, a skilled manual worker living on the outskirts of Phnom Penh in Cambodia, was laid off along with over 50 colleagues following the economic difficulties of the textile plant where she'd worked for over 10 years. "The director told us that orders had halved in six months. With three children, all we have left is my husband's construction work salary. Life's going to get very difficult."

These three situations in three different regions of the world have a single origin: the financial crisis, which originated in the United States. Surprisingly, it affected most world financial markets almost simultaneously, then turned into an economic crisis in many countries. Recovery has been rocky at best, and has led to questions being raised not only about the financial markets and the behaviour of banks, but also globalisation itself. Until now, it could be said that the imbalances and instability caused by globalisation were the inevitable reverse side of the prosperity brought about by opening borders to trade and capital. The world had already gone through serious financial crises (the 1994 Mexican crisis, the 1997 Asian crisis, the burst of the Internet bubble in 2000, the 2001 crisis in Argentina) at a quickening pace that paralleled globalisation. But they were always limited to one country, or at worst one region. This crisis seems to have vindicated the most virulent critics of globalisation, by endangering the economy on all five continents. This chapter examines the role that globalisation – in particular financial globalisation – played in the crisis.

From the subprime crisis to the global bank bailouts, or how the proliferation of "exotic" securities paralysed banks around the world

Before explaining how this crisis spread around the world in such a short time, let's retrace the sequence of events. The causes of the financial crisis are complex. One of them was the excessive debt burden of Western – and especially US – households, particularly in the last decade. Within this context, the crisis was triggered by the proliferation of mortgage loans – the famous subprime loans – granted to low-income households. What was so specific about them? High interest rates and long repayment periods, as they targeted modest households with a relatively high risk of default. In order to attract clients, interest rates were very low at the beginning, then increased significantly after a few years. In the early 2000s, at the height of US growth and confidence in traders, subprime credits were very popular. Nearly six million, mostly low-income US households, were on the receiving end of these loans.

But these subprimes were converted into securities, which were mixed with other secured mortgage loans and traded on the financial markets. This "securitisation" practice presented the triple advantage of being very profitable for banks, reducing their mortgage credit risks and dispersing the risks throughout the financial system. The practice grew exponentially in the past decade, spurred in particular by a range of political measures (see *From Crisis to Recovery* mentioned at the end of the chapter and in the bibliography). As banks increasingly threw themselves into the race for profitable short-term financial operations, the volume and trading of these securities multiplied.

Because of the way global finance was intertwined, as mentioned in previous chapters, securities linked to subprime loans were accumulated in all the banks and on all the financial markets around the world. The problem came from the fact that many households with subprimes had to default on their loans after a few years, as they could not meet the brutal increase in their monthly repayments. These defaults were amplified by the spike in US interest rates starting in 2004 and by the unexpected fall in real estate prices beginning in 2006. The securities linked to these subprimes quickly lost their value, which is when the complex financial products (which included the securities associated with the subprime loans) showed their truly toxic character. Banks no longer had any confidence in the financial products available on the market and stopped transacting. A gigantic financial paralysis followed, initiated by the inter-banking crisis of July 2007. Major banks found themselves totally or nearly bankrupted.

As early as September 2007, Britain's Northern Rock bank was embroiled in a banking panic as its clients withdrew their savings *en masse* in just a few days. In 2008, several other struggling financial institutions were purchased by others (like Bear Stearns by JP Morgan Chase in March 2008, supported by the US Federal Reserve), nationalised (like Freddie Mac and Fanny Mae), placed under US Treasury guardianship, or bankrupted. On 15 September 2008, investment bank Lehman Brothers' bankruptcy petition triggered emergency interventions on the part of governments to spare other institutions the same fate. In fact, their bankruptcy would have had catastrophic repercussions for the entire economy – implied in the expression "too big to fail", which describes institutions that are so connected to the overall economy that governments can't allow them to go bankrupt.

Government intervention did not stop the financial crisis from affecting the "real" economy. Cascading bank failures led to a credit shortage, which blocked investment and corporate operations, plunging the world into a deep economic recession – the first to touch so many countries simultaneously.

A risk dispersion partly facilitated by the global interconnection of banks and financial markets

What role did financial globalisation, that is to say international capital movements, play in the crisis? Essentially an indirect one. To understand this, let's review three phenomena that occurred simultaneously after the 1970s.

The first dates back to the 1970s, when **companies increasingly resorted to the financial markets (through stocks, bonds, etc.) to fund their activities.** The increasingly important financial markets fed and liquefied the economy. Governments began to favour *laisser-faire* economic theories and minimal regulation of market operations to optimise resource allocation and promote economic efficacy and growth. This meant that all sorts of economic players were gradually able to trade all kinds of financial products on the various financial markets (see Chapter 4).

At the same time, **it became possible to conduct financial transactions on the markets of almost *all countries*,** as governments applied the deregulation theory to both international and national financial operations. Financial borders evaporated. Between 1990 and 2004, total assets held by foreigners more than doubled, from 58% to over 131% of global GDP. Around the world today, one listed company share in four is held by a foreign investor – three times more than in 1990. Financial products have also become more globally mobile, making the risks linked to some products more easily "exportable". This mobility was enhanced by the major banking developments during this period.

Finally, **banks became increasingly "globalised".** First, in the years leading up to the crisis, banks consolidated and internationalised. In the 1990s, governments encouraged domestic institutions to consolidate. Banking giants emerged in several countries and expanded their international activities, sometimes through mergers. In 2000, the British banking consortium HSBC acquired Crédit Commercial de France and imposed itself as the 10th largest global banking consortium in terms of market capitalisation.

Thanks to the generalised decompartmentalisation of financial markets, banks became global players, financing corporate and individual activities worldwide and operating on the world financial markets. As a result, the value of international banking transactions (individual loans, corporate loans, etc.) soared from 6% of global GDP in 1972 to nearly 40% in the early 2000s. In 2005, the total foreign exposure of major banks amounted to 40% of total assets.

Financial globalisation occurred in parallel with the rise of risky financial practices. At the same time as they were conquering the world, banks diversified their activities. To sustain growth and increase revenues, major banks expanded their activities to include all financial transactions, even the most speculative and risky ones. They became multi-specialised groups operating in retail banking and traditional products (corporate and individual loans, bank accounts, etc.) as well as in the financial markets (asset management, advising companies on stock transactions, etc.).

To reduce the risk of stocks and bonds losing value (since securities are characterised by their volatility) and hedge against the risks inherent to financial speculation, banks created increasingly complex financial products and hedging instruments – the infamous derivatives. These types of product (among others) allowed them to sell a portion of the risky subprime securities. "Little by little, bankers morphed from takers and dividers of risk into mere risk brokers", summarises economist Olivier Pastré. The derivatives market reached dizzying heights. Meanwhile, the banks were taking more and more risks while removing these risks from their balance sheets, as banking rules then allowed them to do. This explains in part why in 2006, half of all US individual loans were granted without any prior income verification.

It can be said that the unprecedented interconnectedness of global banks and financial markets furthered the dispersion of toxic products to banks around the world and aggravated the geographic reach of the crisis. Yet the globalisation of banks and financial markets isn't in itself the cause of the crisis. In fact, it permitted several decades of global growth by multiplying financing opportunities in the real economy. Another aspect of financial globalisation cultivated the bubble that led to the crisis – imbalances in capital flows between emerging countries and developed countries, which we'll cover a little later.

Financial globalisation also fostered several decades of global growth

The crisis shouldn't overshadow the positive effects of opening national borders to capital flows. Without the free movement of capital gradually introduced in the 1970s, foreign investments, corporate loans, and international finance would not have fertilised industry and new economic activities in a growing number of countries. Global liquidity has never been so important and available (see graph, Panel A). This has allowed the most ambitious projects to emerge. Increased cross-border capital flows resulted in a lower cost of capital (the more plentiful the cash, the easier it is to finance projects at least cost), higher investment growth and considerable productivity gains.

This means that financial globalisation has helped contain inflation in Western countries for over 10 years. Some consider this one of its chief merits. International capital flows ensure relatively constant and abundant liquidity, which allows banks to maintain low interest rates. This is what most of the world's central banks did from the late 1990s onward: interest rates have fallen constantly since 1989 (see graph, Panel B).

Add to this the benefits linked to the globalisation of trade which, as we've seen, promoted imports of inexpensive goods from developing countries due to their low-cost labour and economies of scale. This has also contained inflation. As a result, prices for a range of consumer goods have dropped. Clothes cost less than they used to in most European countries. Lower prices for communications, electronic or household goods, mobile telephones and computers have allowed the less affluent to access new technologies, while new applications and services have enriched the consumer landscape and created new jobs. It's true that prices haven't dropped in all areas and all countries. Some food products in particular have seen alarming price increases. But overall, prices have remained stable or decreased.

Developing countries particularly benefited from the free movement of capital. As we've seen in previous chapters, this is at the core of development in emerging countries, even if they paced the opening of their markets according to their different needs and stages of

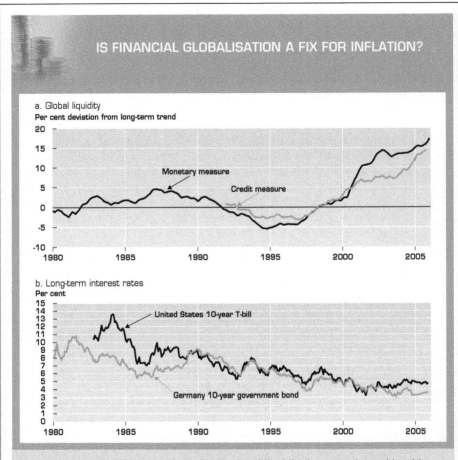

IS FINANCIAL GLOBALISATION A FIX FOR INFLATION?

a. Global liquidity
Per cent deviation from long-term trend

Monetary measure

Credit measure

b. Long-term interest rates
Per cent

United States 10-year T-bill

Germany 10-year government bond

From the mid-1990s onward, available global liquidity increased considerably, mainly thanks to financial globalisation. Some believe this led to reduced interest rates and therefore facilitated credit and economic activity. The 2007-08 financial crisis called this model into question by highlighting the imbalances underlying this abundant liquidity.

Source: World Bank (2006, *Global Economic Prospects 2007: Managing the next Wave of Globalization*, World Bank, Washington, DC, p. 15.

development. International capital flows allowed these countries to receive vast amounts of FDI and to finance their economic activity. These flows also allowed them to build up vast currency and savings reserves, which in turn gave them some protection to weather the grave crises they went through in the late 1990s.

That said, this financial prudence was also partly to blame for the imbalances that laid the groundwork for the current world crisis. Besides risk contagion throughout the world banking systems, one aspect of financial globalisation is more deeply at fault: imbalances in financial flows among great economic powers. This aspect of financial globalisation is one of the most deep-rooted causes of the financial crisis. The subprimes were just a trigger.

Excessive borrowing facilitated by imbalanced capital flows between emerging and developed countries

A closer examination of international capital flows over the last decades shows that the abundantly available liquidity that encouraged borrowing and risky banking practices resulted from a considerable imbalance in financial flows between emerging countries and major Western powers.

As we've seen, the financial crisis was triggered by the inability of many US households to repay their mortgage loans, which reduced to zero the value of the associated mortgage-backed securities. The gravity of the financial paralysis that occurred almost simultaneously worldwide can be explained by the dizzying amounts reached by these products and by the opaque covering of securities linked to them. How could these credits and securities reach such heights?

For years, Western and particularly US households borrowed from banks to buy the expensive televisions, cars and homes synonymous with the American way of life, gambling on a constant rise in real estate prices. This borrowing frenzy was facilitated by very low US interest rates over a period of several years. This was partly the intention of the US Federal Reserve (the US central bank) and the US government, which wished to trigger economic recovery through consumption after the Internet bubble burst in 2001. But the low interest rates were also the "mechanical" result of the influx of capital from emerging countries into the US financial system.

For approximately two decades, the free movement of goods and capital allowed these emerging countries to accumulate considerable (mostly dollar) currency reserves, thanks to their exports, and to invest their gigantic trade surplus in Western economies. Some of these investments consisted of purchases of US Treasury bonds, which were considered particularly stable. This was done mainly through national investment funds (sovereign wealth funds) some of which (as in the United Arab Emirates) are larger than the economies of some developed countries (see graph). Other surpluses were

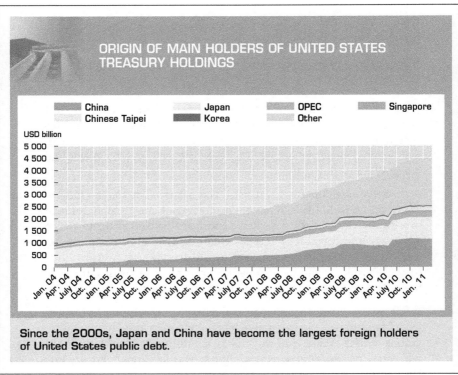

ORIGIN OF MAIN HOLDERS OF UNITED STATES TREASURY HOLDINGS

Legend: China, Japan, OPEC, Singapore, Chinese Taipei, Korea, Other

Since the 2000s, Japan and China have become the largest foreign holders of United States public debt.

Source: "Financial Market Trends", *OECD Journal,* Vol. 2008, No. 94, p. 113, OECD, Paris.

StatLink ⌐⌐ *http://dx.doi.org/10.1787/888932780247*

invested in the capital of major Western companies. The resulting ample liquidity, both in US government coffers and Western financial markets, helped keep interest rates down, spurring Western households to borrow and accumulate debt beyond the capacities of the financial system.

This led many economists to say that emerging countries financed US household debt for over 20 years. Some see this as a negative consequence of financial globalisation. But is the free movement of capital in question, or is it the fact that this free movement isn't generalised? This question – which also partly determines how to respond to the crisis – is the subject of debate. (See the conversation with Adrian Blundell-Wignall at the end of the chapter.)

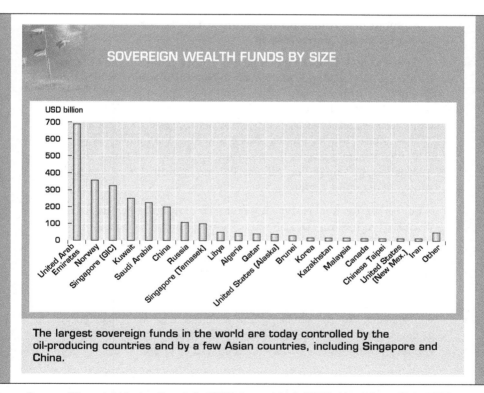

SOVEREIGN WEALTH FUNDS BY SIZE

USD billion

The largest sovereign funds in the world are today controlled by the oil-producing countries and by a few Asian countries, including Singapore and China.

Source: "Financial Market Trends", *OECD Journal*, Vol. 2008, No. 94, p. 121, OECD.
StatLink ᵐˢ⁵ᵐ *http://dx.doi.org/10.1787/888932780266*

Rules, yes, but at what level?

"The stresses of globalisation are visible everywhere. Ultimately, if the politicians want the liberal market system to work, they will have to make multilateralism work."

Philip Stephens, *Financial Times*, 18 September 2008

Even though financial globalisation has yielded many benefits over the past 20 years, the 2007-08 financial crisis revealed major malfunctions, both in banking activities and financial market operations as well as in the highly imbalanced capital flows between emerging countries and Western countries. The free movement of capital across borders should not necessarily mean a total absence of rules.

A global co-ordination framework to manage banking and financial transactions

Given the gravity of the financial crisis, governments were not content to bail out or provide guarantees to banking institutions teetering on the brink of bankruptcy. They also tried to prevent recurring crises, by addressing the failures of the financial system. To do this, they demonstrated political will, especially with regard to international co-operation. They formulated this will within the framework of the G20, whose emergence as the successor to the G8 and first forum of international co-operation reflects the new political and economic weight of emerging countries.

Following the successive G20 summits (London and Pittsburgh in 2009, Toronto in June 2010 and Seoul in November 2010) a number of measures were taken simultaneously. For example, the United States, the European Union and Japan have all introduced reforms allowing them better control of hedge funds, which contributed to inflating the financial bubble. Other projects have been launched by the G20: bonus limits, bank accounting rules, derivative transaction controls, etc. But they are being implemented in national legislations at varying speeds, with significant differences between countries. Global co-ordination is still fragmented and lacking.

And yet co-ordination is particularly crucial. Financial activity is very largely internationalised. Discrepancies in legislation can reduce the most effective domestic legislation to nothing. This is what motivated the reinforced role of the Financial Stability Forum, renamed in 2009 the Financial Stability Board (FSB). The FSB, which brings together the financial authorities of 23 countries (including representatives from the central banks and finance ministries, as well as several international and financial organisations) aims to improve international co-operation in the field of regulation, supervision and control.

The Basel Committee, comprising representatives from central banks and supervisory authorities of a number of countries, plays a similar role, but limited to the banking sector. Yet the crisis revealed not only the insufficiency of the "Basel II" regulatory framework established in 2004 to channel banking risks, but also the fact that it *exacerbated* these risks through its accounting rules. The Basel III protocol, scheduled for implementation early in 2013, lays down rules to solve this conundrum. What's more, following the financial crisis, the Basel Committee expanded in March and June 2009 to include representatives from 27 countries to further harmonise banking rules.

Some international co-ordination regarding banking and financial regulation is taking place, then, even if the substance and harmonisation of the rules, as well as their application, still need improving.

Reform the international monetary and financial system to correct imbalances

Reforms upstream of measures regulating banks and financial markets are going to be needed to resolve the financial imbalances between emerging countries and Western countries, which caused the excessive US household debt. The necessary solutions are still being discussed, but two questions dominate: reforming the international monetary system and managing capital flows.

For many observers, the fact that China and other emerging Asian countries control their currencies (and set their levels) while Western countries let their currencies float against each other (the value of the currency fluctuates according to offer and demand) biases globalisation, since it promotes their exports and exacerbates the trade deficit and household debt of other countries. The solution would be for major emerging countries (including China) to allow their currency more flexibility, in the spirit of the generalised currency floating system characteristic of the post-Bretton Woods era. While the economy is certainly greatly globalised, in some respects it continues to operate at multiple speeds (see the conversation below with Adrian Blundell-Wignall).

The debate on the control of capital flows is more controversial. Some believe that the crisis justifies a return to much stricter government control of capital flows. That's the fondest wish of economists Jean-Hervé Lorenzi and Olivier Pastré, as stated in a 2008 article in *Le Monde* newspaper entitled "A New Bretton Woods". Others believe on the contrary that China, which in addition to controlling its currency also controls capital flows from international markets, has distorted globalisation. For the authors, all countries should fully play the game of free movement, while controlling more strictly some banking and financial market activities (see below).

It's an open debate, but whatever the outcome, "world governments cannot afford to maintain the *status quo*", as OECD Secretary-General Angel Gurría declared repeatedly in the wake of the crisis. Yet these fundamental imbalances are still not resolved, and some see them as major risk factors in any future new global crisis.

A conversation

Adrian Blundell-Wignall, Deputy director, Directorate for Financial and Enterprise Affairs, OECD

"The problem of financial globalisation is that it currently features both rigid and supple elements. Some countries control exchange rates and capital flows. Others allow free markets. This gap engenders structural weaknesses."

Some believe the 2008 financial crisis is the first truly global crisis. Is globalisation responsible for this crisis?

Distortions at the level of global regulation, not the globalised markets, are the main cause of the crisis. But the globalisation process was not undertaken in a sufficiently balanced manner.

Meaning?

Imagine a dam above a village. The reservoir fills with water. But the walls of the dam are badly constructed. They have weaknesses. When the water pressure becomes too high, the dam gives way at these more fragile areas. The water ends up destroying everything. The rising water is the prosperity generated by globalisation. The defective walls are the regulatory frameworks on several levels. The problem of financial globalisation is that to this day, it features both rigid

and supple elements: some countries control exchange rates and capital flows, while others allow free markets. This gap engenders structural weaknesses.

Why is there such a gap?

In 1973, when developed economies instituted a floating currency exchange system, a country like China weighed less, economically, than Australia. While Beijing maintained a fixed exchange rate system for its currency, this was relatively insignificant to the world economy. But in the meantime, some of these countries began to industrialise. Their economic weight is now greater than that of the United States. Under these conditions, Beijing's fixed exchange rate throws the world economy completely off balance. These past years, the Yuan has been dangerously under-evaluated. The US trade deficit compared with China has worsened for that reason. In addition, thanks to their fixed-rate system, some Asian and Middle Eastern countries have been able to accumulate enormous financial reserves. They have recycled liquidity in the very open US economy. The influx of liquidity pushed US interest rates down and inflated the real estate bubble. The United States had only two possible choices: allow the trade deficit to deepen, or increase interest rates. But this latter option would have meant entering wilfully into a recession.

A conversation *(cont.)*

No government wants to do that. So the US deficit continued to widen, compared with emerging countries.

China isn't solely responsible for this imbalance – or is it?

Alan Greenspan, the previous president of the Federal Reserve Bank, found a convenient justification for his lax monetary policy. He spoke of a productive revolution. For him, a new era had opened with the advent of globalisation and Asian industrialisation. We were massively importing Chinese products. It was the Wal-Mart effect [Wal-Mart is the largest US distribution chain, renowned for its very competitive pricing]. The US market was open. Inflation was contained. But all that was set up at the price on the one hand, of a gigantic trade deficit and on the other hand, of an astronomic hike in financial asset prices. It was more comfortable to believe in the productive revolution, but economic laws are what they are. Clearly, Alan Greenspan was wrong.

Should China have been forced to comply with the same rules as other countries in terms of opening its capital market?

Emerging countries should have been associated more with the decisions of the major international economic institutions. For example, they should have obtained the same number of votes at the International Monetary Fund (IMF). In the end, Western countries should have implemented better regulation and better governance that did not create distortion. At the same time, we should have included emerging economies in the decision-making apparatus of the global financial system. Of course, that entailed giving up something, but in my opinion that was the way to go.

During the Asian and Russian crises of the 1990s, shareholders withdrew capital very suddenly. Many blame the IMF for encouraging developing countries to liberalise their capital market too soon. Didn't China, India and a few others do the right thing by locking their systems?

Free trade provides some prosperity, but there is a price to pay. When a country's trade surplus translates into deficits among its trading partners, these deficits must be financed. That's when free movement of capital is required. The impact of FDI on Chinese growth will gradually decrease, as happened in Japan and Western Europe after a period of very strong growth in the 1950s and 1960s. When that stops, you wonder what to do. The industrialisation phase ends and you have to invent something else. That's when you need to open your financial markets, to fuel economic innovation. China will probably not be able to escape this. But China controls capital flows and the value of its currency. Foreigners cannot buy Chinese companies or invest freely in the stock market. If the United States used the same method to stop Chinese operators from buying US assets and converting their yen into dollars, China could no longer sell anything anywhere. Ultimately, this isn't an option.

As soon as a problem crops up in one area of the system, it contaminates the entire system in a split second. Isn't that the problem of financial globalisation today?

I don't agree. It's as if you said that to fight an epidemic of bird flu, you have to remove the air around us, because it transmits the virus. If you have a major solvency crisis in an institution that is present around the world, will it have repercussions on the rest of the system? Of course. But globalisation isn't the cause of the problems. Their root is this generalised insolvency.

Shouldn't we provide security systems to avoid problems spreading throughout the financial world? Like ships, which have airtight compartments...

If we had sensible fiscal and macroeconomic policies, opening financial markets would contribute to global prosperity. To go back to the ship analogy, it's better to have a good radar system and a good navigator.

If globalisation isn't responsible, what do you believe were the causes of the systemic crisis in 2008?

It's a combination of factors. First, the banks changed the economic model. In the past, they took deposits and accumulated them in their accounting balances. They added a bit of capital to that and then lent money. Banks were like paternalist enterprises; they were not caught up in a logic of strong growth at any cost.

A conversation *(cont.)*

But towards 1995, stock valuation began to be more important than the rest. Managers started receiving very large bonuses – *stock options* – based on enhanced shareholder value. They had to boost return on investment. Banks then expanded their activities as investment banks. In the 1990s, intense lobbying succeeded in allowing major banks to develop this kind of activity, which has the advantage of not being subject to prudential capital controls [rules that aim to minimise a bank's risk of insolvency]. Keeping to those rules is expensive. For the banks, that cost equates to a tax. Freed of that cost, they were able to carry out increasingly profitable, but increasingly risky activities. The problem came from these highly risky and volatile investment banking activities.

Consider the domino effect on the banks first hit by the 2008 financial crisis. It all began with the investment bank Bear Stearns, followed by Lehman Brothers, Merrill Lynch, Citigroup and UBS. Finally, AIG, an insurance company, was dragged down by its subsidiary, a London investment bank. In each case, the fall was the consequence of the banks' changed economic model and the intensification of their investment banking activities.

You said that the problems resulted from defective regulation and economic policies. Why didn't we predict the excesses that undermined the banks' activities?

The major US banks used to earn a living selling mortgages to two institutions supported by the US government, Fanny Mae and Freddie Mac. But in 2004, the US regulatory agency limited their capacity to respond. Investment banks played a major role in transforming mortgage assets into investment products that they could then sell to third parties. But they did so in the context of the "American dream", which was supposed to allow all Americans – even the poorest – to own their own home. The products were toxic. So much for failed economic policies.

In 2004, the Basel Committee on Banking Supervision, which sets banking supervisory rules worldwide, voted for the new "Basel II" arsenal of solvency rules. These rules will probably be the shortest-lived regulatory framework in history. Their goal was to make banks more solvent, but they had the opposite effect. Basel II prompted some banks

to reduce their capital in order to increase their yield per share. In addition, regulation encouraged them to take more risks. At a certain point, the crash becomes inevitable and contagion spreads to the rest of the world economy. But again, the problem isn't the air we breathe. The problem comes from the infected chicken coop.

What aspects of the financial globalisation process should be corrected?

Clearly, we need international co-ordination. There's a need and a place for a flow of aid and loans to developing countries. Global co-ordination requires inclusiveness, with an equal number of votes for all.

The globalisation process has been too imbalanced. We can't continue to export and tap into the resources made available by global capital markets without accepting that this is a two-way process. All the economic actors must follow the same rules. That said, I think the global financial system today needs to be more flexible. It should certainly not go back to market protectionism.

So you're not in favour of a stricter supervision of capital flows worldwide?

No. The Bretton Woods model isn't a panacea. In the 1970s, the prices set by the Organization of Petroleum Exporting Countries (OPEC) tripled, which caused a major crisis. The Bundesbank did not wake up one day in 1973 believing that we should let exchange rates float. Germany was losing gold to the United States. There was the Viet Nam war to be financed, etc. The world has always experienced shocks; they did not suddenly arise from globalisation and the free movement of global capital. At the time of the OPEC crisis, there was this strict framework which some still dream of today. The result was that we had 10 years of negative stock returns and massive inflation. People who had fixed-interest investments saw their capital evaporate in three or four years because inflation reached 20%. They lost some of their retirement savings. The Bundesbank did not help to stop Bretton Woods through some sort of ideal, but because it had no choice. The lack of flexibility made the framework economically unviable. Without flexibility, the system can't be robust to shocks.

Find out more

On the Internet

OECD work on the financial markets is available at *www.oecd.org/finance*.

Publications

Financial Markets Trends: This half-yearly publication offers regular updates on the trends and perspectives of the major international financial markets and the main financial markets of the OECD and beyond. See *www.oecd.org/daf/fmt* (in English only).

From Crisis to Recovery: This *OECD Insights* analyses the roots of the 2007/08 crisis and describes how it contaminated the real economy and how the repercussions of the Great Recession will continue to be felt in years to come.

Des subprimes à la récession: Comprendre la crise (From Subprimes to Recession: Understanding the Crisis) (2009): This simple and clear work published by *La Documentation française* and *France info* explains the various stages of the crisis, its practical repercussions on households and companies, and the actions of central banks and governments. It also covers the aftermath of the crisis and the reforms required to avoid a recurrence.

Malaise dans la mondialisation (Malaise in Globalisation), *Questions internationales*, No. 34, November-December 2008: This publication from *La Documentation française* features clear and in-depth analyses of matters related to the crisis and financial globalisation, such as the transformations of the international monetary system since the 19th century, the subprime crisis and its consequences, the integration of stock markets, the growing role of financial markets in the world economy, whitewashing and international financial crime, and the internationalisation of public debt. The articles are written by economists (such as Jean-Hervé Lorenzi, Olivier Pastré and Dominique Plihon), as well as analysts and experts from banks (such as BNP Paribas) and public organisations (such as the Financial Action Task Force).

Alternatives économiques : Spécial crise (Economic Alternatives: Special Crisis Issue), No. 274, November 2008: In this special issue of the economic monthly magazine, economists Michel Aglietta, Christian Chavagneux and Sandra Moatti explain some triggers of the crisis, such as the "debt machine", the government bailouts of the major banks, the financial regulation projects and the crisis of an unequal growth model.

On the Internet

The USD 1.4 Trillion Question: In this *Atlantic Online* article written in the early stages of the crisis in January 2008, economist and former White House economic adviser James Fallows explains very clearly the mechanisms through which China massively invests the surplus deriving from its trade surpluses in the United States, thus contributing to the dangerously high debt of US households. *www.theatlantic.com/magazine/archive/2008/01/the-14-trillion-question/6582*.

General conclusion

Is economic globalisation an opportunity or a risk? Several of its risks have been singled out since the early 1990s, notably the rising inequality it seems to bring in its wake, among countries and social groups (globalisation is sometimes rightly seen as benefiting the powerful and crushing the weak). It is also blamed for the environmental impacts owing to the unbridled consumerism it promotes. To these dangers, we can add those related to the financial, economic and social crisis of 2007-08, which weakened domestic economies overly dependent on globally interconnected banks and financial markets. This crisis in particular highlighted the risks inherent to globalisation. So, has globalisation run its course?

In the wake of the continuing world crisis, the term "deglobalisation" has become widespread – first to describe a real slowing down of trade in the early days of the crisis, then as a call for increased protectionism against potentially catastrophic contagion from financial and economic hiccups. But all the figures have disproved the idea of "deglobalisation", since international trade has resumed at high speed. As for a return to protectionism, economies are so intertwined, with intermediary goods and services accounting for over half of total trade in goods and services, that a step backward appears, if not impossible, at least very risky. Most governments have resisted the temptation to resort to protectionism, whose potential damaging effects became apparent in the 1930s. Governments seem to consider that "deglobalisation" would be riskier than globalisation.

This is particularly true for emerging countries (some of which probably no longer merit this qualification), for which globalisation has been a real opportunity in the last two decades. After a short-lived weakening at the height of the crisis, the Chinese economy quickly resumed growth rates of around 10% per year. Buoyant exports and the presence of emerging countries on all the global markets have played, and will continue to play, a crucial role in this growth.

Have the risks of globalisation shifted during this period from developing countries – now emergent or "convergent" – to developed economies? Most Western workers justifiably feel threatened by the key asset of emerging and developing economies: low-cost labour. But for most of them, globalisation has nevertheless been an opportunity. As new markets and new needs arose, so too did new professions and new jobs. Furthermore, the integration of emerging economies into global markets pushed the prices of numerous goods and services downward for Western households. The great challenge for developed countries is firstly to ensure that some of their workers undergo retraining and secondly, to orient education and training towards the most promising industries.

The environment is only indirectly linked to globalisation. The negative aspects of the human ecological footprint are partly linked to production and consumption models that are currently being reconsidered – mostly in Western countries, but also in (for instance) China or Brazil. It remains that in many developing countries, environmental preoccupations are still considered a luxury. Perhaps one way to foil the risks of globalisation consists in ensuring some complementarity among countries, in the spirit of the public aid for development discussed at the great climate change conferences of Copenhagen in 2009, Cancun in 2010, and Rio+20 in 2012.

Globalisation is neither dangerous nor beneficial in and of *itself*. What matters is how it can be supported to mitigate its risks and seize its opportunities. Governments must pay renewed attention to their role in regulating, preventing and managing economic ups and downs, which spread much more easily. The financial sector seems particularly in need of regulation, even if the forms this should take and effective solutions are still being discussed. Governments, which have been preoccupied with restoring public finances damaged by the crisis and paving the way back to growth and employment, have been slow to adopt measures aimed at better channelling of finance and avoiding financial bubbles and risky behaviours.

Many co-operation mechanisms were in place well before the crisis. One of the major roles of the OECD is to support governments in these types of initiative. The organisation will continue to do so with renewed vigour. If we want to avoid a recurrence of devastating crises and increased environmental degradation, tomorrow's globalisation can only be achieved through co-operation.

References

Chapter 1

BBC (2008), "Global Poll Suggests Widespread Unease About Economy and Globalisation", BBC Website, *www.bbc.co.uk/pressoffice/pressreleases/stories/2008/02_february/07/poll.shtml*.

Bhagwati, J. (2004), *In Defense of Globalization*, Oxford University Press, New York.

Brunel, S. (2007), "Qu'est-ce que la mondialisation?" (What Is Globalisation?), *Revue Sciences Humaines*, No. 80, March 2007, special issue.

Issenberg, S. (2007), *The Sushi Economy: Globalization and the Making of a Modern Delicacy*, Gotham Books, New York.

OECD (2007), "Making the Most of Globalisation", *OECD Economic Outlook*, Vol. 2007, No. 1, OECD, *http://dx.doi.org/10.1787/eco_outlook-v2007-1-39-en*.

Stiglitz, J.E. (2002), *Globalization and its Discontents*, W.W. Norton and Co., New York.

Stiglitz, J.E. (2006), *Making Globalisation Work*, W.W. Norton and Co., New York.

Wolf, M. (2005), *Why Globalization Works*, Yale Nota Bene, New Haven and London.

Chapters 2 and 3

Bordo, M., M. Taylor and J. Williamson (2003), *Globalization in Historical Perspective*, University of Chicago Press, Chicago.

Braudel, F. (2000), *Civilisation matérielle, économie et capitalisme (Material Civilisation, Economics and Capitalism)*, 1979, new edition, LGF, 3 Vols.

Chanda, N. (2007), *Bound Together: How Traders, Preachers, Adventurers and Warriors Shaped Globalization*, Yale University Press, Michigan.

Maddison, A. (2001), *The World Economy: A Millennial Perspective*, OECD Development Centre Studies, OECD, Paris, *http://dx.doi.org/10.1787/9789264289987-fr*.

Maddison, A. (2003), *The World Economy: Historical Statistics*, OECD Development Centre Studies, OECD, Paris, *http://dx.doi.org/10.1787/9789264104150-fr*.

Toussaint, E. (2008), "La mondialisation de Christophe Colomb et Vasco de Gama à aujourd'hui" (Globalisation from Christopher Columbus and Vasco de Gama to Today), 6 February 2008, *www.cadtm.org/La-globalisation-de-Christophe*.

Turner, P. and J.P. Tuveri (1984), "Effet des restrictions à l'exportation sur le comportement des entreprises japonaises" (Effects of Export Restrictions on the Behaviour of Japanese Firms), *OECD Economic Review*, No. 2, second quarter, OECD, *www.oecd.org/dataoecd/62/5/2501796.pdf*.

Chapter 4

World Bank (2007), *Global Economic Prospects 2007: Managing the Next Wave of Globalization*, World Bank, Washington, DC.

Benhamou, L. (2005), *Le grand bazar mondial (The Great World Bazaar)*, Bourin Éditeur, Paris.

Bensidoun, I. and D. Ünal-Kesenci (2007), "La mondialisation des services : De la mesure à l'analyse" (Globalisation of Services: From Measurement to Analysis), CEPII, *www.cepii.fr/francgraph/doctravail/resumes/2007/dt07-14.htm*.

Berger, S. (2005), *How We Compete: What Companies Around the World Are Doing to Make it in Today's Global Economy*, Currency/Doubleday, New York.

Cheung, C. and S. Guichard (2009), "Understanding the World Trade Collapse", *OECD Economics Department Working Papers*, No. 729, OECD Publishing, Paris, *http://dx.doi.org/10.1787/220821574732*.

Friedman, T.L. (2005), *The World Is Flat: A Brief History of the Twenty-First Century*, Farrar, Straus and Giroux, New York.

Ghemawat, P. (2007), *Redefining Global Strategy: Crossing Borders in a World Where Differences Still Matter*, Harvard Business School Press, Boston.

IMF (International Monetary Fund) (2007), *Reaping the Benefits of Financial Globalization*, Research Department, IMF.

Initiative Neue Soziale Marktwirtschaft und der Internalen Handels-
kammer (ICC) Deutschland (2007), *Globalisierung verstehen: Unsere
Welt in Zahlen, Fakten, Analysen*, Hamburg, 2007.

Kose, A. *et al.* (2006), "Financial Globalization: A Reappraisal",
Working Paper WP/06/189, 2006, IMF, Washington, DC.

Kose, A. *et al.* (2007), "Financial Globalization: Beyond the Blame
Game", *Finance and Development*, March 2007, Vol. 44, No. 1,
IMF, Washington, DC.

Love, P. and R. Lattimore (2009), "International Trade: Free, Fair
and Open?", *OECD Insights*, OECD, Paris, *http://dx.doi.org/
10.1787/9789264060265-en*.

OECD (2006), *International Migration Outlook 2006*, OECD, Paris,
http://dx.doi.org/10.1787/migr_outlook-2006-en.

OECD (2008), *The Internationalisation of Business R&D: Evidence,
Impacts and Implications*, OECD, Paris, *http://dx.doi.org/
10.1787/9789264044050-in*.

OECD (2010), *Trade and Economic Effects of Responses to the
Economic Crisis*, OECD, Paris, *http://dx.doi.org/10.1787/
9789264088436-in*.

OECD (2010), *Measuring Globalisation: OECD Economic Globalisation
Indicators 2010*, OECD, Parishttp://dx.doi.org/10.1787/
9789264084360-in*.

Rivoli, P. (2005), *The Travels of a T-Shirt in the Globalised
Economy*, Wiley & Sons, Hoboken.

UNCTAD (United Nations Conference on Trade and Development)
and L. Berger (2004), "Services Offshoring Takes Off in Europe:
In Search of Improved Competitiveness", UNCTAD, Geneva.

UNCTAD (2005-08), *Prospects for Foreign Direct Investment and the
Strategies of Transnational Corporations*, UNCTAD, New York.

UNCTAD (2007), "Globalization of Port Logistics: Opportunities
and Challenges for the Developing Countries", UNCTAD,
Executive Summary, 10 December 2007.

UNCTAD (2007), *World Investment Report*, UNCTAD, New York.

UNCTAD (2008), *World Investment Report*, UNCTAD, New York.

Chapter 5

Aykut, D. and A. Goldstein (2006), "Developing Countries MNEs: South-South Investments Come of Age", *OECD Development Centre Working Papers*, No. 257, OECD, Paris, *http://dx.doi.org/10.1787/245230176440*.

Dedieu, F. (2010), "Idée reçue : La mondialisation aide à sortir de la pauvreté" (Idée Reçue: Globalisation Provides an Exit from Poverty), *http://lexpansion.lexpress.fr*.

Gibbon, P. and S. Ponte (2005), *Trading Down: Africa, Value Chains, And The Global Economy*, Temple University Press, Philadelphia.

OECD (2008), *Growing Unequal? Income Distribution and Poverty in OECD Countries*, OECD, Paris, *http://dx.doi.org/10.1787/9789264044197-en*.

OECD (2010), *Perspectives on Global Development 2010: Shifting Wealth*, OECD Development Centre, OECD, Paris, *http://dx.doi.org/10.1787/9789264084742-fr*.

OECD (2010), *Latin American Economic Outlook 2011: How Middle Class is Latin America?*, OECD, Paris, *http://dx.doi.org/10.1787/leo-2011-en*.

Prahalad, C.K. (2004), *The Fortune at the Bottom of the Pyramid: Eradicating Poverty Through Profits*, Wharton School Publishing, USA.

Rajan, R.G. and L. Zingales (2000), "The Great Reversals: The Politics of Financial Development in the 20th Century", *OECD Economics Department Working Papers*, No. 265, OECD, Paris, *http://dx.doi.org/10.1787/371486741616*.

Rodríguez, J. and J. Santiso (2007), "Banking on Development: Private Banks and Aid Donors in Developing Countries", *OECD Development Centre Working Papers*, No. 263, OECD, Paris, *http://dx.doi.org/10.1787/044646710662*.

UN (United Nations) (2008), *Development-Oriented Policies for Socio-Economic Inclusive Information Society, Including Access, Infrastructure and an Enabling Environment*, Report of the Secretary-General, UN, Geneva, 25 March 2008.

UN (2010), *Millennium Development Goals*, 2010 Report, UN, New York.

Zeng, M. and P.J. Williamson (2007), *Dragons at Your Door: How Chinese Cost Innovation is Disrupting Global Competition*, Harvard Business School Press, Boston.

Chapter 6

Jules, R. (2010), "La nouvelle carte salariale émergente" (The Emerging Wage Board), *La Tribune*, 14 June.

Keeley, B. (2007), "Human Capital: How What You Know Shapes Your Life", *OECD Insights*, OECD, Paris, *http://dx.doi.org/10.1787/9789264029095-en.*

Koulopoulos, T.M. (2006), *Smartsourcing: Driving Innovation and Growth Through Outsourcing*, Platinum Press, Avon, Mass.

Molnár, M., N. Pain and D. Taglioni (2007), "The Internationalisation of Production, International Outsourcing and Employment in the OECD", *OECD Economics Department Working Papers,* No. 561, OECD, Paris, *http://dx.doi.org/10.1787/167350640103.*

OECD (2007), "Globalisation, Jobs and Wages", *OECD Policy Brief,* July, OECD, Paris, *www.oecd.org/employment/employmentpolicies anddata/38796126.pdf.*

OECD (2007), *Staying Competitive in the Global Economy: Moving Up the Value Chain*, OECD, Paris, *http://dx.doi.org/10.1787/9789264034259-en.*

OECD (2008), "The Social Impact of Foreign Direct Investment", *OECD Policy Brief,* July, OECD, Paris, *www.oecd.org/els/40940418.pdf.*

OECD (2008), *OECD Employment Outlook 2008*, OECD, Paris, *http://dx.doi.org/10.1787/empl_outlook-2008-en.*

OECD (2010), *OECD Employment Outlook 2010: Moving Beyond the Jobs Crisis*, OECD, *http://dx.doi.org/10.1787/empl_outlook-2010-en.*

OECD (2011), *Divided We Stand: Why Inequality Keeps Rising*, OECD, Paris, *http://dx.doi.org/10.1787/9789264119536-en.*

Chapter 7

Gillespie, B. and X. Leflaive, (2007), "Innovation, Globalisation and Environment", *OECD Observer*, No. 261, OECD, Paris, *www.oecd observer.org/news/fullstory.php/aid/2240/Innovation,_globalisation_and_the_environment.html.*

IPCC (2008), *Climate Change 2007: Synthesis Report,* IPCC, Geneva.

OECD (2007), *Climate Change in the European Alps: Adapting Winter Tourism and Natural Hazards Management*, OECD, *http://dx.doi.org/10.1787/9789264031692-en*.

OECD (2008), "Environment and Globalisation: Background Report for Ministers", Background reading documentation from "Meeting of the Environment Policy Committee (EPOC) at Ministerial Level", 26-29 April 2008, *www.oecd.org/dataoecd/ 3/59/40511624.pdf*.

OECD (2008), *Environmental Outlook to 2030*, OECD, Paris, *http:// dx.doi.org/10.1787/261365884052*.

Chapter 8

Blundell-Wignall, A. (2009), "The Financial Crisis and the Requirements of Reform", speech presented during the session "Restoring Confidence in Financial Systems" at the OECD Forum 2009, 23-24 June, *www.oecd.org/document/54/0,3746,in_21571361_ 41723666_42942201_1_1_1_1,00.html*.

Blundell-Wignall, A. and P. Atkinson (2010), "Thinking Beyond Basel III: Necessary Solutions for Capital and Liquidity", *OECD Journal: Financial Market Trends*, Vol. 2010/1, OECD, *http:// dx.doi.org/10.1787/fmt-2010-5km7k9tpcjmn*.

Blundell-Wignall, A., P. Atkinson and S.H. Lee (2009), "The Current Financial Crisis: Causes and Policy Issues", *OECD Journal: Financial Market Trends*, Vol. 2008/2, OECD, *http://dx.doi.org/10.1787/fmt-v2008-art10-in*.

Cohen, D. (2009), "Sortir de la crise" (Getting Out of the Crisis), *Le Nouvel Observateur*, 3-9 Septembre 2009.

Couderc, N. and O. Montel-Dumont (2009), "Des subprimes à la récession : Comprendre la crise" (From Subprimes to Recession: Understanding the Crisis), *La Documentation française*/France Info, Paris.

The Economist, (2010), "Not All on the Same Page", *The Economist*, 1 July 2010, London, *www.economist.com/node/16485376?story_ id=16485376*.

Fallows, J. (2008), "The $1.4 Trillion Question", *The Atlantic*, Boston, *www.theatlantic.com/magazine/archive/2008/01/the-14-trillion-question/6582.*

International Centre for Financial Regulation (2011), "China, the G20 and Global Financial Governance After the Crisis", ICFR Breakfast Briefing, *www.icffr.org/assets/pdfs/March-2011/China,-the-G20-and-Global-Financial-Governance-aft.aspx.*

Jones, H. (2010), "G20 Progress on Financial Regulation", Reuters, 23 June 2010, *www.reuters.com/article/idUSLDE65M0YN20100623.*

Keeley, B. and P. Love (2011), "From Crisis to Recovery: The Causes, Course and Consequences of the Great Recession", *OECD Insights*, OECD, Paris, *http://dx.doi.org/10.1787/9789264077072-en.*

MacGuire, P. and N. Tarashev (2008), "Global Monitoring with the BIS International Banking Statistics", Bank for International Settlements, *Working documents*, No. 244, January 2008.

OECD (2009), "OECD Strategic Response to the Financial and Economic Crisis: Contributions to Global Effort", Document prepared for the OECD Meeting of the Council at Ministerial Level, June, OECD, Paris, *www.oecd.org/economy/42528786.pdf.*

OECD (2010), *The Financial Crisis: Reform and Exit Strategies*, OECD, Paris, *http://dx.doi.org/10.1787/9789264073036-en.*

Questions internationales (2008), "Malaise dans la mondialisation" (Malaise in Globalisation), *Questions internationales*, No. 34, November-December, Special issue, Paris.

ORGANISATION FOR ECONOMIC CO-OPERATION AND DEVELOPMENT

The OECD is a unique forum where governments work together to address the economic, social and environmental challenges of globalisation. The OECD is also at the forefront of efforts to understand and to help governments respond to new developments and concerns, such as corporate governance, the information economy and the challenges of an ageing population. The Organisation provides a setting where governments can compare policy experiences, seek answers to common problems, identify good practice and work to co-ordinate domestic and international policies.

The OECD member countries are: Australia, Austria, Belgium, Canada, Chile, the Czech Republic, Denmark, Estonia, Finland, France, Germany, Greece, Hungary, Iceland, Ireland, Israel, Italy, Japan, Korea, Luxembourg, Mexico, the Netherlands, New Zealand, Norway, Poland, Portugal, the Slovak Republic, Slovenia, Spain, Sweden, Switzerland, Turkey, the United Kingdom and the United States. The European Union takes part in the work of the OECD.

OECD Publishing disseminates widely the results of the Organisation's statistics gathering and research on economic, social and environmental issues, as well as the conventions, guidelines and standards agreed by its members.

OECD PUBLISHING, 2, rue André-Pascal, 75775 PARIS CEDEX 16
(01 2011 11 1 P) ISBN 978-92-64-11189-9 – No. 58919   2013-07

Lightning Source UK Ltd.
Milton Keynes UK
UKHW021119160721
387270UK00005B/103